THE SPAS OF ENGLAND

The
Spas of England

PETER J. NEVILLE HAVINS

LONDON
ROBERT HALE & COMPANY

ISBN 0 7091 5264 7

Robert Hale & Company
Clerkenwell House
Clerkenwell Green
London EC1R OHT

Filmset by Specialised Offset Services Ltd, Liverpool
and printed and bound in Great Britain by
Redwood Burn Limited, Trowbridge and Esher

CONTENTS

1	Sprites, Saints and Superstition	11
2	The Early Spas	20
3	The Challengers	34
4	The Victorian Spas	57
5	Spa People	72
6	The Coastal Spas	103
7	Spa Architecture	113
8	The Cures	132
9	The Social Round	145
10	The School Towns	161
11	And So To?	180
	Index	187

ILLUSTRATIONS

Between page 64 and 65

1 An eighteenth-century print of Bath by Thomas Loggon
2 The Pantiles at Tunbridge Wells in 1699
3 & 4 (left) Beau Nash (right) Beau Brummel
5 The Royal Crescent, Bath
6 The Roman Bath and Abbey, Bath
7 The Pump Room, Bath
8 The Pump Room at Bath, 1798, by Rowlandson
"It shocks me to see them look paler than ashes,
And as dead in the eye as the bust of Nash is,
Who the evening before were so blooming and plump,
I'm grieved to the heart when I go to the pump."
9 A nineteenth-century satirical drawing of the votaries of hydropathy
10 The Cross Bath, Bath, 1738, by L. Fayram
11 Fountains in the Promenade, Cheltenham
12 The Rotunda, formerly part of the Montpellier spa, Cheltenham
13 The Raven Hotel, Droitwich, remodelled by Corbett c. 1830

Between pages 128 and 129

14 & 15 In the early nineteenth century, Bath (above) was still very close to the country – a characteristic which later spa promoters such as Smedley at Matlock Bath (below) took advantage of

16 The spa at Scarborough

17 The Pump Room, Harrogate

18 The more domestic architecture of the Royal Crescent, Brighton

19 The Royal Pavilion, Brighton

20 The Pantiles, Tunbridge Wells, still well patronised by the Victorians

21 St Ann's Well, Malvern

22 Clifton, Bristol. The mud of the River Avon polluted the original hot well, thus leading to the demise of the spa but the Grand Spa Hotel, on the top of the hill, contains the Clifton Assembly Rooms dating from the new spa which succeeded the old Hotwells spa

23 The nineteenth-century 'pepper pot' above the mineral spring discovered in 1840 at Tenbury Wells, now a café

24 Modern remnants of the spas (above) The Flask in Flask Walk, Hampstead, London's principal spa, and (below) tasting the waters at Cheltenham

PICTURE CREDITS

Radio Times Hulton Picture Library: 1, 2, 3, 4, 8, 9, 10, 14, 20; Kenneth Scowen: 5, 6, 11, 18, 19; Geoffrey Wright: 7, 12, 13, 17, 21, 23; F. Leonard Jackson: 15; John Edenbrow: 16; G. Sherren: 22, 24; *The Times*: 25

ACKNOWLEDGMENTS

I am indebted to a large number of people whose help has made this book possible. In particular I would like to acknowledge the assistance of Dr H.L. Lehmann F.R.I.C. of the Surrey Archaeological Society for information on Epsom Wells; M.G.R. Bourne for permission to use notes from an unpublished thesis on Droitwich Spa; Martin P. Barnsley, F.L.A; Law Library/Bodleian Library Oxford; Miss O.S. Newman and the staff of Salop County Library, Shrewsbury; Mrs M. Pringle, Local History Librarian, Borough of Cheltenham Public Libraries; C. Batt A.L.A., Area Librarian Brighton Public Libraries, Mr S.P. Burstow, Honorary Archivist, Brighton College; Mr L. Bamberger, Museums Curator, Margate; Mrs G. Manchester, Publications Officer, North Wales Tourist Board; Mr I. Burton, Local History Librarian, Buxton; Mr D. Tyler, Pier and Foreshore Officer, Southend-on-Sea; Mrs H. Wood, Assistant Amenities Officer, Leamington Spa; Alan Dearden F.L.A., Assistant County Librarian, Scarborough.

TO JILL, ALBERT AND TIGGY

1

Sprites, Saints and Superstition

The English spa town, the spa of Beau Nash and Jane Austen, is basically of eighteenth-century origin though some centres, such as Bath, considerably pre-date the era, while others, such as Worcestershire's Tenbury Wells and the great northern spa of Harrogate, were very much later creations.

Yet to refer to the creation of the English spa in this sense is to risk dangerously confining its consideration to a social and architectural period which many of the eighteenth-century spas themselves in many ways greatly pre-dated.

Many English spas enjoyed an existence as watering-places throughout most of the medieval period and Bath, as we all know, was the thriving centre of the spa business as long ago as Roman times. In medieval times many springs and wells were attributed with healing properties, these being generally ascribed to the influence of a particular saint. Yet, obviously, the waters had been there before the introduction of Christian symbolism and very often a well or spring had earlier been the site of a Celtic shrine under a succession of gods and religious codes.

Water, in an appropriate environment, seems always to have been capable of raising awe in the sub-conscious – even in England, where it often pours on us in all too plentiful abundance. But water gushing up from some unknown underground source often awakens a very natural sense of wonder – even now there are few who can fail to be moved by a visit to the watery grandeur of Somerset's Wookey Hole, even allowing for the bric-a-brac of nearby commercial exploitation. By the same token it is small wonder that so many public houses in the hillier parts of Britain are called the Rock and Fountain in alcoholic commemoration of Moses and the miracle of the Rock. This apart, water was early given a symbolic use in Christian ritual in the rite of baptism; and when the various kingdoms of Anglo-Saxon England were first converted to Christianity there could have been little hesitation in the minds of the early missionaries that previously pagan water shrines should be converted to serve the needs of the new religion. (If old habits die hard their various justifications could thus be said to be somewhat irrelevant).

Two of the most important medieval European watering-places were to be found in Britain, namely at Walsingham, Norfolk and Holywell, Flintshire. At the shrine sited near the well dedicated to Our Lady of Walsingham, a vision of the Blessed Virgin Mary was said to have appeared to a local swineherd in 1061, a spring erupting to mark the spot. The spring was soon to acquire more than a mere local reputation for healing and was later to be administered by the Augustinian monks of the nearby monastery. Over the centuries prior to the Dissolution – and for some time afterward – numerous cures were to be recorded. However, these must be attributed either to faith or divine intervention as scientific analysis in later centuries was to reveal that the water was devoid of any medicinal properties.

St Winifred's Well at Holywell was said to have burst forth when the ground had opportunely opened to swallow a lecherous Celtic prince who had been pursuing a chaste Christian maiden – the Winifred of the title – with fairly obvious intent. Prior to his sudden disappearance the rebuffed prince had lopped off Winifred's head, which was later restored so that she could go on to become the Abbess of Gwytherin. St Winifred's Well was destined to survive in popularity long after the iconoclasm of the Reformation and, although an eighteenth-century bishop of St Asaph's poured scorn on the supersitions of those who continued to use it, his words had little effect. Even today it still retains its devotees.

But these two cure centres were both in the uncomfortable British – and later English – tradition of cold water. Bath, the Aquae Sulis of the Romans, was an altogether different story with its thermal waters catering not so much for religious zeal, but for luxurious wallowing – something for which the latter-day Romans especially seem to have developed a peculiar knack.

That the mineral waters of Bath's hot springs were in use long before the arrival of the Romans and their architectural grandure seems to be born out by the legend of the Celtic King, Bladud, the father of the original of Shakespeare's King Lear. Bladud was afflicted with leprosy and quitted the court to live as a swineherd. He appears to have noticed that some of his diseased charges had been cured by wallowing in the muddy waters of the swamp that occupied the site of the present-day baths. He was only too willing to follow their example, was ultimately cured himself and can therefore be said to have laid the earliest foundations of Bath's reputation as a cure-centre.

It may well have been that Bath's waters were the object of Celtic religious veneration in pre-Roman days, for the thermal waters of the region were dedicated to the goddess Sul. When the Romans arrived they merely translated the existing place-name – Aquae Sulis – and, associating Sul with their own goddess of medicine, gave a double-barrelled dedication to Sul Minerva.

Under the Romans Aquae Sulis was to be developed almost purely as a recuperative centre and was one of the few towns established by them in Britain that did not originate from essentially military or economic reasons. In the days when the empire was a smooth-running piece of administrative machinery Aquae Sulis was to gain a reputation throughout the northern provinces and visitors to its waters came from as far away as Gaul and Franconia.

In the north Midlands Buxton was also to develop as a spa under the Romans – and, to a far lesser degree, this may also have been the case with Droitwich. Buxton has some Roman remains and there is some evidence to suggest that it may have been used as a rest centre for soldiers from the frontier legions who would certainly have used the thermal waters.

But it was Bath which was to enjoy pre-eminence. Unlike the other settlements it not only developed as a Roman town in its own right but stood at the edge of a region which was to be extensively developed by Roman colonia – settlements for retired soldiers. The climate also favoured the settlement of wealthy Romans or, more probably, of Romano-Celts who had made their fortunes under the empire, in villas scattered around the nearby Cotswolds. Then again there was the nearby garrison-town of Glevum (Gloucester) and these three factors assured it of a local prosperity. Given the creation of good communications with London and the south-east coast and the way was open for visitors from across the seas.

In many ways Roman Bath, though it was later to be neglected to the point where it sank back under its sea of swamp, was the real forerunner of the later English spa. The Romans, of course, already had their native models to base it upon and at these medicinal bathing had become only one of the features of 'the cure'. The whole rather hedonistic set-up would have found very little favour with the Christian authorities who came to administer England's watering-places in later centuries.

Recuperation was the major function of the baths, but it had early been recognised as a major precept that 'all cure and no play' made Gaius a dull Roman. In the light of this the baths had become the centre of social life, a place where administrators from Londinium and Ebocorium could recover their bureaucratic spirits with a little healthy dissipation. The baths were the centres of gaming, athletic contests, poetry readings (which were almost the equivalent of today's pop concerts), plentiful drinking (not of water), not a little vice and a modicum of bathing.

In time, of course, the Romans left – their empire racked by invasion and civil war, – and probably, for a little time, the baths of Aquae Sulis continued to be used by the local Romano-British population. But, when the Saxons spread their advance westward, they seem to have showed little liking for organised bathing. They certainly disliked and distrusted anything Roman, even to the extent of building their original settlements well away from earlier Roman sites and, as a mark of the unsettled nature of the times, generally made sure, for defensive reasons, that they were also far removed from the Roman roads.

At Aquae Sulis the baths were deserted and sank back to the point where their site once again resembled that which had seen Bladud and his swine. In later days a town gradually re-established itself, its waters having some reputation for healing. But it was not destined to prosper for many years and in the reign of William II was burned in the civil war between William and his brother Robert, Duke of Normandy. In the same reign the Bishop of Bath and Wells purchased Bath from the king, together with baths and abbey and some years later Alexander Neckham, the philosopher-scientist, was to maintain that the warm waters were good for "age's ills" and a variety of other complaints.

But the thermal waters did not really again begin to become popular until the fifteenth century – and were then hardly to be invested with the trappings of elegance which contributed so largely to the glories of eighteenth-century Bath. 'Custom' decreed that all bathers take the waters naked – largely, it would seem, for the benefit of the onlookers who crowded the baths and who were not above stripping anyone who attempted to enter the waters semi-clad. Added to this, anyone who succeeded in outwitting the Bath naturists could be fined, again 'according to custom'. All this was too much for Thomas Beckington, Bishop of Bath and Wells, who, in 1449, ordered that all bathers, but especially it would seem adolescent boys and girls, should bathe decorously clad. The only exceptions to the new ruling were to be children who had not yet reached the age of puberty. The bishop's ruling, however, was apparently little heeded – medieval bishops laid down the law no more effectively than modern ones – and Bath's reputation for bawdy licence amid the warm waters was hardly calculated to make it the mecca for the jaundiced nobility.

As at Bath so throughout Britain the water spirits and deities of pagan times were ultimately banished – often to be replaced by Christian saints, many of whom had no real connection with water. There was, however, a widespread belief that anything connected with a good or holy person – even if by no more than the later attachment of their name – would automatically take some of this goodness to itself and later transfer it to anyone who came into contact with it. For similar reasons do teenagers treasure mementoes of pop-stars and sporting personalities.

Wells with religious associations were very often dedicated to St Brigid – or to St Bride, which was another version of the name. But this was usually the case of the Church having to make the best of an existing situation, for wells and springs with such a dedication had often earlier been associated with the Celtic goddess Brigantia. Brigantia was the goddess of arts and crafts and just how she came to be mixed up with so much water-worship is something of a mystery.

Medieval England abounded with holy wells which had once been pagan sites, though they were also especially numerous in the country's 'Celtic fringe', in Cornwall; Cumberland, Northumberland and the Welsh border region. Legends were often associated with the healing wells, such as that dedicated to St Neot at the Cornish village of that name. St Neot was reputed to have been the brother of Alfred the Great and to have given up the bustle of ninth-century religious life to retire here as a hermit attended by one servant. He was said to have a very soft spot for animals and once, when a hunted stag took refuge with him near the well, he is reputed to have reproved the pursuing hounds with the result that they slunk away duly abashed. On another occasion the saint was feeling somewhat peckish but was suffering from a bout of debility. His servant thought that he might appreciate a little fish, caught a couple of trout from the nearby stream, boiling one and broiling the other. Feeling pleased with his resourcefulness the servant duly presented them to St Neot – but Neot was not amused. Far from it in fact, and he ordered the servant to return them to the river. The servant, who after all, had gone to a lot of trouble, returned them with reluctance. But he was duly impressed when, no sooner had the fish entered the water, they swam off downstream for all the world as if they had never been boiled or broiled at all. It was St Neot's general reputation for sanctity that was later to provide the well with an associated reputation for being able to cure most diseases.

From pagan times many wells had been decorated with

flowers and garlands at thanksgiving festivals, for the wells
and the springs which fed them were almost literally the life-
blood of many a local community. Well-dressing still survives
in Derbyshire, where it was long ago given a Christian
significance. But the practice was once common in many other
areas of the country. At Droitwich well-dressing was practised
at St Richard's Well – though only incidentally in connection
with the water. It was this St Richard – originally Richard de
la Wyche, later bishop of Chichester – who had once restored
the salt springs of the town after they had run dry and it was
believed that if the well subsequently dedicated to him were
not honoured then the supply would again dry up. Indeed,
when during the Commonwealth, the custom was
discontinued, the well did dry up. Heedless of Puritan edicts
to the contrary the well-dressing was revived and the waters
again began to flow. Needless to say, as Droitwich is no longer
a centre of the salt-trade, no-one bothers to dress St Richard's
well today.

Another spa which had a connection with water-legends in
the days before it was due to find a more fashionable fame was
that at Gilsland in Cumberland. Here there is said to have
been a well especially noted for its curative waters. A local
speculator bought the surrounding land and erected a house
over the well-head with the intention of selling the waters.
Almost immediately the waters are said to have dried up and
did not flow again until the offending house was pulled down.
This legend does not seem to have affected the latter
development of the spa.

Many wells in medieval England were devoted to the cure of
one particular disease – but, to judge by the number that were
reputed to cure poor eyesight alone, medieval Englishmen
must have been hard put to it to avoid bumping into one
another. There were Eye Wells at Malvern, at Ludlow – the
Bubbling Well and at Bradford – the Holy Well. Herefordshire
was one county that was particularly favoured with them.

A large number of wells which were claimed to cure almost
all known diseases were reputed to have been the site of
particularly inexplicable miracles. One such was that of St
Kenelm near Romsley, Worcestershire. The well was said to

mark the spot of the murder of the child-king of Mercia, discovered after a dove had delivered a scroll revealing its whereabouts on the High Altar of St Peter's as the Pope was celebrating Mass.

A rather more home-grown miracle was associated with St Catherine's Well, Newark, Nottinghamshire, which was said to mark the site of the murder of Sir Everard Bevercote by his companion Sir Guy Saucimer. The murder had been committed in a fit of temper and afterward Sir Guy was duly repentant. But he was forced to suffer from leprosy as a penance. Later he bathed in the well and the leprosy ceased to afflict him. A chapel was built enclosing the well and dedicated to St Catherine and the well-shrine rapidly acquired a reputation for being able to cure many types of illness.

It was asking a lot of the English (and the Celts, for that matter) to throw up the practices and beliefs of centuries in the name of the Protestant Reformation. Throughout the country attempts were made, on the orders of Henry VIII – who had himself, in 1511, made a much publicised pilgrimage to the waters of Our Lady of Walsingham – to stamp out the religious practices associated with the holy wells. Small wonder that the ordinary people were confused and continued to use the wells, although the images and relics were to be taken away and the majority of well-side chapels demolished. A number were later to be bought up by the rising 'Tudor gentry', who entered the ranks of the landed aristocracy very much as a result of Henry selling off so much of his newly-acquired Church lands. If a 'holy well' was to be found on a tenant's land it was quite often the case that, as a good infant capitalist, he mounted a local publicity campaign and would succeed in reviving at least a small part of its former pilgrimage trade. From his point of view the well was not so much a spiritual asset as a financial one.

However, over the years following the Reformation, many wells while still being used did, to a large extent, lose their old religious associations. One notable exception to the trend was St Winifred's Well which has maintained its religious associations right up to the present day and, in the latter years of the last century, was to be found making a serious bid to be considered as 'the English Lourdes'. This was hardly good topography, though perhaps it was thought that 'the Welsh Lourdes' would not sufficiently attract the credulous English.

But, in general, the association with saints was to be largely lost over time. A large number of wells gradually ceased to be used – though many hundreds did not. Many of those that remained came to be valued locally purely for their medicinal qualities – real or imagined – though some element of religious veneration still clung to some. By the mid-seventeenth century it may broadly be said that England's remaining wells were of three main types, those which still retained a strong religious association but which were generally falling out of all but local favour, those local wells valued largely for medicinal values but with only a local reputation and those which had medicinal value and which were already beginning to attract a wider recognition, such as the waters of Tunbridge, Harrogate and Epsom.

It was to be these three, and others like them, that were destined to develop as the first English spas at the beginning of a process that was finally to come full-circle in the Regency recreation of the long-buried social life of Roman Bath.

2

Early Spas

Of the four major spa centres of seventeenth century England only one, Bath, did not originate from post-Reformation times. Each of the others owed their development to the discovery of their waters in Tudor and early Stuart times, those of Harrogate being discovered in 1571, of Tunbridge in 1606 and of Epsom in 1618. These, of course, were not the only spas which functioned at the time. But they were the only ones which really maintained momentum and which have left behind them visible remains of their spa-centre life.

One centre which could have, perhaps, have been expected to take its place alongside those already mentioned was Oxfordshire's Astrop. This enjoyed the life of a booming little spa from roughly Restoration times until the mid-eighteenth century. Its well was dedicated to St Rumbold – the baby saint – and possessed a healing tradition dating back to the early middle ages. In 1688 its medicinal qualities were brought to the notice of a local physician and further support was given by a doctor Radcliffe from nearby Oxford. When Celia Fiennes visited it on one of her hyperchondriacal 'spa-crawls' she found it already vying with Tunbridge and sporting a gravel walk between high, trimmed hedges, an Assembly Room and a Music Room. In the early years of the eighteenth century there was, in season, dancing, cards and a public breakfast every Friday and a ball every Monday. It attracted the fashionable patrons of London society and was already one of the most well-known social centres in the country. The waters, however, began to lose some of their reputation, the tide of Astrop's short-lived popularity died out and the spa was to revert to the backwater it had been before the 'learned physicians" discovery.

Roughly at the same time that Astrop was first being developed as a spa the Clifton Hot Wells, situated in the Severn Gorge near Bristol, sprang up to a rather more durable fame. The wells were discovered at the foot of the St Vincent Rocks at a spot where hopeful and deluded local people often went prospecting for diamonds. John Evelyn, the diarist contemporary of Pepys, commented on the qualities and warmth of the waters which broke surface here along the same line of geological faulting as those at Bath. The waters were claimed to be especially beneficial to consumptives and those suffering from various respiratory disorders. A spa developed, which was to remain fashionable as long as nearby Bath was popular. As Bath began to decline, the Clifton Hot Wells, which had tended to depend on the same clientele, also began to wane. By the mid-nineteenth century Clifton had changed from a spa to a fashionable suburb of Bristol – which it still is.

Near to London, Barnet grew into a brief spa town roughly at the same time as Epsom and was to enjoy the passing patronage of Samuel Pepys – who, amongst other things, was somewhat addicted to passing fads in medicine. In London itself there were Sadler's Wells, discovered by Thomas Sadler in 1683 and now the site of the famous theatre, and there were other centres at Sydenham, Islington and Clerkenwell. Many of these metropolitan spas were to enjoy only a brief and fleeting fame but others, such as Sadler's Wells itself, were developed as pleasure gardens and lasted, as such, well into the nineteenth century.

With the exception of Harrogate all the major spas of this period were to be found in the south. But it was Harrogate which was the first spa creation of the time and, indeed, the resort was to earn itself the title of the 'first English Spaw'. Its waters were discovered in 1571 by William Slingsby, a local landowner, who noticed that those of its first well, the Teewit Well, bore a marked resemblance to those at Spa in Germany where he had seen service as a soldier in the Continental wars. It was not, however, until 1596 that it was first described as resembling Spa when Dr Timothy Bright published a treatise praising the qualities of its waters.

The development of Harrogate in its early years was to be in marked contrast to that of the three major spa towns of the south, in that the huddle of cottages that comprised the actual spa scarcely developed at all, almost all the benefits of its new-found property going to the nearby market-town of Knaresborough. While it was the wells of Harrogate that brought in the visitors it was the town of Knaresborough which first developed as the spa.

Not until the end of the eighteenth century did the Harrogate 'season' come to be fully located in Harrogate itself. Before this there had been a period of well over a century while the actual spa sought to take over as the 'spa centre' from its ancient neighbour. One result of all this was an additional spate of building in Knaresborough itself. Many early Georgian houses still remain together with the 'oldest chemists' shop in the country' – it is a rather depressing fact that spa towns always seem to have more than their fair share of chemists' shops.

The spa on the 'desolate moors' grew gradually – inns springing up which were described as looking more like 'gentlemen's country seats'. Celia Fiennes had spent most of her Harrogate stay at Knaresborough and many visitors in the years afterwards did so too. But increasingly, as facilities slowly improved, people preferred to stay in Harrogate itself and, in time, Harrogate came to dominate 'in season' while Knaresborough would reassume its old authority at its close. By the beginning of the nineteenth century Harrogate was poised to usurp the former position of Knaresborough altogether and the subsequent development of Harrogate itself will be related in later chapters.

Chronologically it was the waters of Tunbridge Wells which were next to be discovered – and, for many years, Tunbridge was to be simply refered to as 'The Wells'. Here the waters first attracted the notice of Dudley, Lord North whilst staying with Lord Abergavenny at his hunting lodge, Eridge House. North, who had some inkling of their properties, sent samples of the water to London for analysis and it was subsequently reported that they were good for various disorders including melancholia – a pronounced disease of the younger Stuart gentry – and infertility. Their fame spread slowly, but, in

1630, Tunbridge was to receive a visit from Queen Henrietta Maria, who was recuperating after the birth of the troublesome Prince James. She and her courtiers must have enjoyed themselves in a place where, it was later to be said, 'the Horizon is fill'd with an inexhaustible series of Odoriferous and Fragrant Effluviums'. Tunbridge as a town – or even a village – was then scarcely in existence and the Queen's party were accommodated in tents and temporary wooden buildings. But, besides their taking the waters, the party was to enjoy the usual masques and elaborate dances of the Court. The Queen seemed well-pleased with it all – but it was obvious that better provisions for accommodation and amusement had to be made if Tunbridge was to take off as a fully-fledged centre of fashionable diversion.

Some improvement had been made by the time Charles II's Queen, Catherine of Braganza, came to Tunbridge in 1663, to be followed, a short while later, by Charles himself and most of those ennobled ladies who sought his more intimate favours. By now the ground near 'The Wells' had been levelled and trees had been planted to form an avenue then known as the Upper and Lower Walks and which were destined to later develop into the famous Pantiles. But, although the king and his immediate company could now be housed, most of the other fashionable visitors still had to make shift with tented and temporary accommodation – which was probably quite all right as long as it didn't rain. Two years later, in 1665, Charles and his frolicking court again came to Tunbridge – this time to escape from plague-infested London. It was this second visit that laid the true foundation of Tunbridge's Restoration fortunes, for the Royal visit to 'The Wells' now became an annual affair. Assured of regular patronage, shops, houses and inns sprang up to cater for the influx of visitors – although a good part of the infant town was to be burnt to the ground in a disastrous fire in 1687.

The early *al fresco* way of living at The Wells and the general dispensing with Court ceremony by those there was soon to give Tunbridge a reputation for licentiousness and drew the censure of Puritans who described the medicinal wells as 'the waters of scandal'.

The waters were to be popularised by various medical writers, most notably by a Dr Patrick Madan. They were claimed to be good for almost any complaint, especially infertility, but the waters were considered so strong that it was considered dangerous for them to be taken by those suffering from fevers, consumptive disorders or by the aged.

Royal visitors continued to give the town their patronage, including the king's younger brother, Prince James and, later, his daughter Princess Anne (later to be Queen) who was to prove the town's most generous benefactor. By the reign of William and Mary, Tunbridge, besides its numerous houses and inns, possessed two substantial coffee-houses, lotteries and hazard-rooms, bowling greens and – the thing that that no spa then or since seems to have been able to do without – a large number of chemists' shops. But, despite this development, it was still very much a rural place. When Princess Anne visited Tunbridge her young son, the infant Duke of Gloucester, slipped and fell while playing on one of the grass walks. She gave £100 to have it paved with the square baked Pantiles that have given their name to the town's most distinctive architectural feature – it is only fair to say that most of the Pantiles have, in fact, been repaved, and that only a handful of the original tiles now remain.

Tunbridge was now the leader of fashion outside London and a lot of querulous noises were made by the town when local spas in London itself appeared to be attempting to set up in competition. Particular displeasure was directed to the opening of Islington Spa. But the London spas could not really compete. They were all too near the city to ever hope to remain as exclusive as 'The Wells' and the nobility and fashionable soon deserted these places as the middle-class began to flock to them, returning to the rarified atmosphere of relatively isolated Tunbridge.

The social hey-day of Tunbridge belongs to the period roughly spanned by the late seventeenth and early eighteenth centuries – though, rather strangely, it was not to acquire most of its distinctive spa architecture until the Regency period. Tunbridge and Bath came to complement each other for their seasons did not clash, and the link was to acquire even greater significance when, in 1735, Beau Richard Nash became Master of Ceremonies at Tunbridge whilst retaining the same position at Bath. It was now generally considered that no one had really taken 'the cure' – in the social rather than the medical sense – unless they had visited both places. The resort was visited by Garrick, Johnson – and presumably by Boswell – Richardson and Sir Joshua Reynolds amongst a long list of celebrities.

As a spa, Tunbridge survived into the early years of the nineteenth century though, by then, most of its former clientele, like that of Bath, had deserted it in favour of up-and-coming Brighton. Its Regency buildings, many of which like Claverley Crescent, were designed by Decimus Burton, were designed, in retrospect, not so much as an addition to the old spa, but rather as the beginnings of its transition to a residential centre. By the mid 1830s this new role had been assumed with confidence and though 'the spa' still had an existence the town had now throughly outgrown its beginnings.

Of the London wells that had most threatened the primacy of Tunbridge that at Epsom was probably the most successful. Given a greater distance from London it is quite likely that it would have developed as the out-of-town Court social centre rather than Tunbridge.

Its origins went back to 1618 when Henry Wicker, a local farmer who was attempting to enlarge an existing water-hole for his cattle, discovered that they would not drink the water it produced. Henry tried the water himself and was soon to discover that, though it might not find favour with the cows, it was to become all the rage with local people who were to claim that it cured gout, liver complaints and much else. The fame of the waters soon spread to nearby London and soon the small village was being inundated by visitors.

Epsom must really have felt it was on the road to fame and fortune when, following the Restoration, it, like Tunbridge, came to be patronised by Charles II and his Court. On more than one occasion he is said to have installed Nell Gwyn at a nearby inn – not wishing to have time hang too heavily on his hands in the evenings.

In the middle years of Charles' reign Samuel Pepys came to Epsom – whose waters, he was later to record, gave him 'many good stools'. But he found the place so crowded that he had to find lodging at Ashtead. Epsom offered most of the fashionable amusements, including dancing, gaming and bowls and quite a few that were not so fashionable – including wrestling, cudgel-playing and hawking. To provide even greater diversion horse-racing was begun on the Downs – and it is from this precedent that we may trace the origins of the present Derby Week.

But, as Samuel Pepys recorded, Epsom was too near London for the Court to feel really comfortable. He found it full of tradesmen and pondered awhile just how they had come by the inclination to visit Epsom and, having come by the inclination, he was to ponder further on how they had come by the money. Epsom was duly to be deserted by the nobility and taken up by the middle-class. Which really meant that, if it sank a little in the social scale, it was still bringing in the money for, in the early years of the eighteenth century, more than 2000 people a day were taking the waters.

But, faced with this daily multitude, Epsom's well could not hope to maintain itself forever. In due time it was to run dry and local businessmen – then as now, the pillars of our society – decided to mount a rescue operation. Under cover of darkness the well was refilled with water from nearby wells which contained only a minimal amount of the valuable 'saline matter'. They argued, perhaps, that no one would notice the difference. Perhaps no one did – for certainly taking the water had become one of the least important things that visitors sought in the town.

In the early-eighteenth century the old well was bought and closed by a Doctor John Livingstone. There had been nasty rumours about the quality of the water and Livingstone considered that the best way to protect their reputation was to let no one taste them at all. This local well-wisher now opened another nearby declaring that its waters were just as good as those of the old – they probably were, though no one will ever know just how much tampering the zealous doctor was to do to these particular waters. Livingstone had grand plans to restore Epsom to its former glory as a leading spa town and resort of the Court and nobility.

In due course, partly as a result of Livingstone's efforts, it made its bid for a new fame with new assembly rooms, gaming rooms and – nothing if not fashionable in terms of late-eighteenth-century social facilities – with an Oriental bazaar. The novelty of the bazaar was enough, for a time, to attract George Augustus, the Prince Regent who, naturally enough in the confused romances of the age, in turn attracted Mrs FitzHerbert to the spa.

But an Oriental bazaar was hardly enough to hold 'Prinny' forever. He began to hanker after a whole Oriental palace – and got one at Brighton. Off he went, trailing his entourage behind him, to spend days drinking sea-water and later, when this seemed rather niggardly, in actually bathing in the sea. Others followed his example – and have been doing so ever since. Epsom as a spa was finished. Its salts continued to be packaged and sent to chemists everywhere – especially to those in spa towns. At Epsom today there is little to recall the days of the spa – apart from the site of the old well, now railed off and from which no one can even attempt to take the waters.

The flight of fashion from eighteenth century Epsom was probably the most abrupt to be experienced by any town which had entertained the pretensions of being a major spa. There remain almost no tangible links today which can associate Epsom with this particular side of its seventeenth- and eighteenth-century life – apart, that is, from its enclosed well.

Such was hardly the case with Bath, the one spa in this particular group which had enjoyed a fitful existence in the years prior to the Reformation. In the early seventeenth century it bid to become an out-of-town centre for England's sluggish, constipated and liverish nobility when it was paid a series of visits by James I's Queen, Anne of Modena. Like all monarchs James wanted an heir to preserve the succession – particularly in view of the troubled state of national affairs at the time. Having been rather slow in producing one Anne was packed off to Bath on the advice of Sir Theodore Mayerne, the Royal physician. In course of time the waters, or other considerations, brought about their due effect. Naturally enough, the burgesses of Bath now vaunted their waters as expeditious in producing offspring. As a result the waters seem to have been crowded with infertile ladies of noble birth busily attempting to speed the arrival of the young nobles who were destined to die in such quantity in the coming Civil War.

Of the five baths the most favoured – and therefore endowed with the greatest social eclat – was the King's Bath where visiting gentry were less likely to suffer from the ribaldry of the citizenry and where there was a certain amount of privacy in the form of a number of arches around the edges of the bath.

Despite the fact that only the Hot Bath was partially covered – which not only removed the embarrassment created by the ranks of spectators who crowded the sides of the other baths and who, judging by a local bye-law, were not averse to throwing dogs into the waters to create a little additional indecorum; but which also shielded the bathers somewhat from the wind and rain that could lash the more open ones – the nobility continued to patronise Bath up to the outbreak of the Civil War. After the Restoration they returned again and a visit by Charles II's Queen, Catherine of Braganza, in 1663, put the royal seal of approval on the place.

Samuel Pepys was of the opinion that the arrangements at Bath were the very opposite of hygienic and wondered if it could really be healthy for so many people to be packed into the same water. But Pepys' opinions did not seem to discourage Charles from bringing his mistressess, the Duchess of Portland and the Duchess of Cleveland to take the waters in 1674 – and no doubt a good time was had by all.

Order was maintained at the King's Bath by a bath-sergeant and the attendants seem to have performed their duties with increasing courtesy – motivated, of course, by self-interest, for the bath attendants made a handsome living from their fees. The season lasted about five months with the lodging-house keepers charging exorbitant prices and netting huge profits. Out of season the town was virtually empty of visitors and had a sense of desolation. But conditions were poor in the extreme – compared to the change that was to have been achieved by the end of the eighteenth century.

Seventeenth-century Bath was still very much a medieval

town – and a medieval provincial town was hardly the creation of the Palladian school of architects. It was enclosed by its wall, had narrow streets, and conditions in many of the lodging-houses were so bad that the walls were painted with a mixture of beer and soot to disguise the dirt of centuries. Given all this it is surprising that anyone bothered to go to Bath at all – hot baths or not.

The change toward the Bath we know today began to take place during the reign of Queen Anne. It was largely precipitated by Anne herself who, as at Tunbridge, was not amused by the lack of amenities. It was during these years that the first Pump Room was built – drinking as against bathing having been very slow to catch on at Bath – and, in 1708, the first Assembly Rooms were erected.

It was during these years that Richard Nash came to the city, at first to act as deputy to Captain Webster who was in charge of the Town Hall gaming tables. When Webster was killed in a duel after an argument at the tables his position fell to Nash who, not unnaturally, made his first action the banning of swords from the gaming rooms.

Just how much of the subsequent elegance of Bath social life was to be directly attributable to Nash's influence is a matter of some dispute. But it was certainly a situation in which order had to be introduced and if Nash had not been there as a titular 'social monarch' then undoubtedly someone else would have had to be found.

Bath was something of a social crucible where the various strata of the English hierarchy melted a little for the duration of their stay, but certainly not to the point where they were beyond resuming their places in the stratum thereafter. There were, on the one hand, the townsfolk themselves, the indigenous poor and the relatively well-off local traders. Then again there were the local gentry, the squirearchy, who would have rarely been in touch with London-based nobility if it had not been for the attractions of the resort. Finally there was the nobility itself, the power-seekers and those who actually possessed power surmounted by the various representatives of the dogged, taciturn, feuding and brilliantly unstable Hanoverian monarchy.

Added to each of these groups – except perhaps the first –

were an enormous league of hangers-on, gamblers, fortune-hunters, rakes, villains, social butterflies, profiteers and speculators in anything from morals to building land. In fact the social composition of fashionable Bath was both very Chaucerian and very modern.

The rise of eighteenth-century Bath was due, very largely, to the influence of two very different men. Richard Nash established himself as the arbiter of elegance in the spa town while Ralph Allen devoted much of his fortune to beautifying it. Allen was a Cornishman whose fortunes were founded on his revolutionary reorganisation of the Royal Mail system. He invested the substantial profits he derived from the implementation of his 'cross-posts system' in land around Bath and in the Bath stone quarries at Combe Down, no doubt with a firm eye to the future development of the town. The development subsequently came and Allen was to do both the Bath of his day and our own an inestimable service when he commissioned John Wood the Elder to undertake the first step towards rebuilding the medieval town in the Classical manner. Wood, a Yorkshireman, undertook his first commission for Allen in 1726 when he added a wing to Allen's town house and the following year was to see him completing the building of St John's Hospital. He was now to begin the building of Queen's Square, which was intended to mark the beginning of the realisation of his concept for the complete re-modelling of Bath as a 'classical' city which would bear comparison with any in Europe. Unfortunately he was not to live to see his work completed – it never was to be – but his son, John Wood the Younger, was later to carry out much of his father's original design.

In the social sphere the regime established at Bath by Richard Nash was to exert a great influence on other spas, most of whom copied it to a considerable degree, Tunbridge almost completely when it imported Nash himself to oversee its summer season. Almost all spa towns now seemed to find it essential to have a Master of Ceremonies of their own and the early sea-side resorts, such as Brighton and Margate, were later to regard, at least in their early years, such a personage as indispensible.

If it was Ralph Allen who provided much of the capital for the creation of the Squares and Crescents of classical Bath it was Richard Nash who not only supervised but, in many cases, was actually responsible for providing the directions in which the occupants of these elegant thoroughfares spent their leisure. Although Nash did, to a certain extent, line his own pocket at Bath, he was not a rich man and was to provide many of the town's original amenities by means of subscriptions. It was subscription payments which were responsible for music in the pump-room, a playhouse, public access to hitherto private walks, assembly rooms and a host of minor details which added to the quality of spa life. He was also responsible for pressuring the local burgesses into paving and cleaning the major roads in the city.

But the 'Beau's' greatest claim to fame was that he introduced an element of decorum into the social confusion that reigned in the social stew of early eighteenth century Bath. Not only were the squires and *nouveau-riche* speculators taken to task for loutish behaviour toward members of the visiting nobility, but the nobility could be equally chastened for snobbishly insulting their social inferiors. Oliver Goldsmith, in his 'Life of Richard Nash', was of the opinion that Nash's regime had been one in which 'regularity repressed pride' and that the introduction of a certain code of ceremony had been the salvation of Bath as a social centre.

The establishment of Bath as a fashionable spa centre was no inconsiderable influence in the rise of a number of other, smaller centres in its neighbourhood. The Clifton Hot Wells, near Bristol have already been mentioned and it is enough to repeat that their fortunes were tied very closely to those of Bath itself. If anything Clifton functioned as an overflow spa to the larger spa and when Bath itself began to decline at the beginning of the nineteenth century Clifton was destined to be swamped by nearby Bristol and its spa functions to sink into oblivion.

Beyond Bath, to the south, Alford, Wells and Holt all made modest bids to enter the spa race – but none were to be really successful. One town which was to achieve a fair measure of popularity, however, was Melksham. Here a pump-room was erected and there was a rash of building that produced some fine Georgian houses. Its visitors seem to have been largely composed of those seeking a further cure after the social whirligig of Bath and it stood in much the same relation to the greater spa as did Clifton. But Melksham's popularity deserted it sooner; it had waned by the end of the eighteenth century and fallen back to its more natural function as a market-town.

Far away from the general spa concentration in the south and west one other spa began to rise to something a little above local prominence at this period – though its real fortunes were not to be founded until the early nineteenth century. This was the mid-Welsh resort of Llandrindod Wells, where the use of its waters was said to date back to Roman days. However, as had been the case with Bath, the medicinal values of Llandrindod's waters had been largely forgotten after the Romans had left and the town did not again begin to profit by them until the end of the seventeenth century.

Llandrindod had iron, sulphur and saline waters and its springs were said to have been known to the Romans as 'Balneae Silures'. Although it achieved a modest local fame in the late seventeenth century it was not to aspire beyond this until the eighteenth. A Mrs Jenkins claimed to have rediscovered the sulphur and saline springs in 1736. A number of cures were soon attributed to the waters and, via articles in the 'Gentleman's Magazine' and similiar publications, Llandrindrod was soon attracting a number of wealthy clients.

As a result of this publicity there was a considerable rash of speculative building. Houses and a sumptuous hotel were built, together with a ballroom and gaming rooms. Later a racecourse was laid out. Llandrindod, however, was to suffer from its sudden mushrooming. Toward the end of the eighteenth century it acquired a reputation for licence and as a centre for debauched dissipation where the young bloods of the English gentry went to do anything but take the cure.

In a gesture of apparent contrition the owner of its hotel had it completely demolished and Llandrindod entered a period of slump from which it was not to revive until the days of the Regency.

In the early nineteenth century a small inn was converted into a hotel, pamphlets again began to praise the local waters and the visitors gradually began to reappear. By the third decade of the century inumerable cottages were offering accommodation, a host of other buildings had been turned into hotels and the Pump Room was doing a thriving trade. The subsequent development of the spa was to a large extent dependent upon the arrival of the Central Wales Railway which, via Craven Arms, provided Llandrindod with a through route to London. It was thus in the Victorian years that the spa reached the height of its popularity and we will turn to it again – and to its Victorian rivals, Harrogate and Buxton – in a later chapter.

3
The Challengers

In the mid and latter years of the eighteenth century a new breed of spa town began to make its appearance and to offer the first effective competition to the hegemony exercised over the fashionable spa industry by Bath and Tunbridge. In the north Scarborough and Harrogate began to rival the spa-dormitory of Knaresborough, whilst in the Midlands Leamington and Cheltenham both began to make inroads into the clientele which had formerly moved almost exclusively between Tunbridge and Bath. Of this new foursome Scarborough emerges as something of a rogue elephant, for it was to be the only one of the new spas which was not to be thoroughly re-vamped as a purely spa resort, the late-eighteenth century passion for sea-bathing pushing it into a far different direction. This being the case, it will be wiser to leave consideration of Scarborough to be included with that of the rise of the other early coastal resorts such as Weymouth and Brighton.

In contrast especially to Bath the new spas were not to be unduly hampered by much earlier development. Although Georgian and Regency façades did not exactly appear overnight the development of the new towns from what had been essentially small rural communities went ahead with both greater rapidity and unity of design than had been initially possible at the older centre. This being so, Cheltenham and Leamington – though Harrogate was a different case and was to develop rather differently – in their central areas, still preserve, without undue modification, the most perfect representations of the Regency English spa.

Cheltenham was the only one of these new towns which had almost totally ignored its local waters before the 'spa fever' of the eighteenth century. Its original well had been 'discovered' in 1716 and the lowly locals who had been using it as an occasional cheap aid in combating rheumatism suddenly found it enclosed, canopied and no longer freely accessible.

Although the medicinal qualities of Cheltenham's waters had drawn comment from Fuller and Campden as early as the sixteenth century, the town was to owe its initial development to one man, Henry Skillicorne. Skillicorne married the daughter of William Mason, who had enclosed the mineral well standing upon his land. For some years Henry Skillicorne, retired Manx sea-captain and merchant, and his wife lived at Bristol; but when William Mason died they took up their landed inheritance and settled at Cheltenham.

The Captain, who had earlier been a frequent visitor to Bath and the Clifton Hot Wells, was to see great possibilities in the Cheltenham well and rapidly developed the intention of making it the focal point for a new spa which, he hoped, would eventually come to rival Bath. Skillicorne undertook various embellishments to the Cheltenham scene, notably in relation to the well itself and in the creation of the long-vanished tree-lined avenue of Well Walk. But, although some visitors were to grace this infant spa at the foot of the desolate Cotswolds, this was the Classical Age – Gothic romanticisms of the Scott/Wordsworth brand still lay far in the future – and the venture was to enjoy only a modest success. The Captain was duly depressed by his apparent failure. When however, in course of time, he died, he was commemorated in the parish church by the longest epitaph in England. It could hardly have been a great consolation.

But the spa had already been visited by such well-known personalities as Doctor Johnson and the composer Handel, and Cheltenham was soon to be looking to an optimistic future forecast by the Captain's son, William. He, as something of a go-getter, was to take up his father's near-abandoned schemes and endow them with renewed vigour.

Under William Skillicorne, Cheltenham slowly began to blossom, though not all its improvements were to be due to his influence. In the mid 1760s the town still possessed only the rudiments of a spa with, besides its well, a temporary theatre housed in a converted barn and two precursors of the later

Assembly Rooms in the form of the Town Rooms presided over by Mrs Jones and the Long Room adjacent to the Well and in the ownership of William Skillicorne.

The two rooms, each vying for the patronage of the same wealthy visitors, produced a natural war for supremacy. The generals in the short-lived campaign both claimed to be Master of Ceremonies for the whole spa, William Miller of the Long Room being a Londoner imported by William Skillicorne, while Simon Moreau of the Town Rooms had been a second-string Master of Ceremonies at Bath, had apparently imported himself and had been adopted by Mrs Jones as her protégé.

The battle was conducted with great bitterness. The ghost of William Miller might still haunt the rooms of the Princess Hall extension to the Ladies' College – the presumed site of the original well and Long Room – still endeavouring to re-establish some of his lost social standing. For some time Miller refused Moreau access to the Long Room, and after this obstacle had been removed, Moreau was to discover that he was still forbidden to taste the waters of the well itself.

But such a dispute could not last indefinitely and it began to be said that such an unseemly public wrangle was damaging to the reputation of the new spa. By the time that George III paid the town a visit in 1788 – and, incidentally, by his very presence, pushed the town into the front rank of spas – the contest seems to have been decided in Moreau's favour. He had by then, become Cheltenham's undisputed Master of Ceremonies responsible, not only for directing its public entertainments, but also for producing the spa's first directories. The fastidious and aesthetic Moreau was to reign until his death in 1810 when he was succeeded by James King, who managed to double his summer functions at Cheltenham whilst remaining Master of Ceremonies at Bath during the winter.

The Miller-Skillicorne combination were to be even more mortified when Thomas Hughes, a clerk who had married a local heiress, erected a new Assembly Rooms on the site of the old Town Rooms, effectively syphoning off a large part of their business. Skillicorne and Hughes, however, did combine, as members of the Cheltenham Commissioners, to ensure that the old Butter Cross and Corn Market in High Street were demolished to improve the Georgian appearance of the thoroughfare and to see that it was subsequently paved and lighted.

As Cheltenham moved into the nineteenth century and the new spa really began to sink roots as a fashionable Regency centre, its social life came to be dominated by the dashing and somewhat ostentatious Colonel William FitzHardinge Berkeley. The Colonel was the first son of the Fifth Earl Berkeley and Mary Cole, but had been born before their legal marriage in 1796. A previous faked marriage had taken place which had evidently been well-enough contrived for Mary to believe it was valid and subsequently for her to naturally assume that her first son would be the rightful heir to the Berkeley estates and title. Thus, in all good faith, William came to accept this position also. Mary, however, was to later learn the true circumstances of her earlier marriage and – being nothing if not the canny daughter of a Bristol butcher later destined to turn down an offer of marriage from none other than the future William IV – she insisted that the Earl go through with a second, valid, solemnisation.

All this was to create problems for William. When the Fifth Earl died William assumed the title, but the matter was later to come before the House of Lords which ruled that the rightful Earl Berkeley was William's youngest brother – actually the eighth in line – Thomas Moreton, who had been born to Mary and the Fifth Earl after their later marriage.

William now adopted the title of Colonel Berkeley, which he held in the Gloucestershire Yeomanry, and his brother refused to accept his inheritance, pledged that he would never marry so as not to pass the title to the estate to his heirs and allowed William to continue to live at Berkeley Castle as though he were still the rightful heir. Such cases of fraternal self-sacrifice are indeed rare.

The Colonel was to give generously to Cheltenham and was a patron of both sport and the theatre – he often appeared on the stage of Cheltenham's 'Theatre Royal' as the leading member of a group of aristocratic players. In 1819 he gave

£1000 which went a long way to seeing the establishment of the famous Cheltenham Races and annually brought more than the usual splash of colour to the spa when, at the close of season, he led the Berkeley Hunt in procession through the streets.

Colonel Berkeley and Simon Moreau were the twin-hubs of Cheltenham's social life but, although Moreau reigned as Master of Ceremonies for almost a quarter of a century, the main architectural survivors of Regency Cheltenham largely belong to the years immediately after his death. Some new building had, however, already taken place by this time, notably the Royal Crescent and a number of palatial houses – the leader here being Bayshill Lodge, originally known as Fauconberg Hall and built for Lord Fauconberg in 1781. Many of the buildings in the High Street, including the Plough Hotel, had also been brought up to date by the addition of Regency façades and the Colonade, later to become the Promenade – surely one of the most evocative thoroughfares in England – was largely in existence. But new building on the grand scale did not really gather momentum until the years immediately following the Napoleonic Wars when, between 1816 and 1818, the town saw its new Assembly Rooms opened by none other than the Duke of Wellington – still mantled in the glory of Waterloo – the opening of the Montpellier Pump Room – now housing a branch of Lloyd's ubiquitous bank – and, in 1818, the completion of the Sherbourne Pump Room, later renamed the Imperial Spa which stood on the site of the present Queen's Hotel.

After Brighton, Cheltenham could well have been described as the 'swinging-city' of the later Regency (1820-1830) and there was one man who certainly considered that it could aspire to still greater heights. Joseph Pitt was a self made man from Cirencester who had first built up a successful legal practice and later moved into the ranks of the landed gentry. His ambition in relation to Cheltenham was not to supplement the already existing spas in the town but to establish Pittville – clutching for immortality – as a new and self-contained spa itself. Initially Pitt hoped that his new creation would feed off Cheltenham's established clientele, but ultimately his aim was to see Pittville rise to the point where it would eclipse the older centre.

Unfortunately for Joseph Pitt his scheme was a rather belated one. New development began in Pittville and the Pittville Pump Room was eventually opened in 1830 after many delays in construction. The Pump Room, which has recently been restored, must rank as Cheltenham's most glorious monument to the Regency spa. But it was never to prove as popular as Pitt had hoped. Pittville was not destined to emerge as a separate entity from Cheltenham but rather to become its suburb. In these circumstances it was too far from the centre of the town for its new Pump Room to become much more than a centre for the occasional special event. This apart, by the time the Pump Room had opened, the general popularity of spas – at least of the Regency type which mixed much pleasure with only a minimal amount of medicinal water – was on the decline. Pittville did not rival Cheltenham, it came too late to really invigorate it and, although this had been far from Joseph's Pitt's intentions, the Pittville Pump Room now seems to have been erected largely as an unconscious memorial to the lost life of Regency Cheltenham.

Yet, although the Pittville pavilion was the last major spa building to be erected in Cheltenham, the town, like so many others, had so established its image that it was well-able to survive as a scaled-down spa-centre well into our own century, the splendour of its buildings at least ensuring that it never completely severed its links with Hygenia. But the town had to change. After the erection of the Pittville Pump Room the spa itself ceased to expand. But the town itself did not and from the late 1830s must date Cheltenham's next phase of development into a slowly expanding residential centre.

This slow change of function was to take place at almost all the larger spas though naturally not to all at the same time, for Cheltenham's Midland rival Leamington did not seriously begin to decline until the early 1850s.

Unlike Cheltenham Leamington's waters had been in use since at least the sixteenth century. But, for many years, the saline waters enjoyed only a local reputation and Leamington was not to see its beginnings as a spa until 1784 when a

Warwick physician, Dr Holyoak, well aware of the financial possibilities in controlling and publicising such waters, offered to purchase Leamington's well-site from its owner, Lord Aylesford. Aylesford turned him down because the doctor's proposals would have entailed excluding the town's poor from the site. But Holyoak's interest showed the way the fashionable wind was blowing and, over the next three decades, Leamington was to expand to the point where it was able to enter the national spa league and, by 1820, it was making a fair bid to be considered its 'most promising newcomer'.

Leamington's spa beginnings were greatly fostered by the discovery, two years after Lord Aylesford had turned down the Warwick doctor's offer, of a saline spring in the grounds of William Abbott. With the aid of Benjamin Satchwell, who belonged to the growing group of writers who passed their time praising spa waters in verse, Abbott lost no time in publicising its cure-all properties, and before long the town was attracting wealthy industrialists from the North and Midlands intent on removing the executive disorders contracted whilst supervising England's industrial revolution. Over the next few years a clutch of other wells were to be discovered around the town, their waters being either saline, chalybeate or sulphurous.

Leamington's spa building, however, did not really begin to get under way until the first decade of the nineteenth century. And it was somewhat aided by the interest of the Prince Regent – a frequent visitor to nearby Warwick Castle – who was present in the town in 1812 for the opening of the aptly named Regent's Hotel on the Parade.

The town's first Pump Room had been erected in 1808 by a consortium of local businessmen and parts of the Parade and Regent's Street were already in existence or in the process of construction. In 1813 the fifth Earl Aylesford was responsible for the erection of an ornate housing at the original well and in 1821 'The Parthenon' – later to be renamed The Assembly Rooms – was opened in Bath Street.

Leamington now possessed the essential elements of a spa and, for the next twenty years or so, the town continued to expand steadily. Most of the town's most celebrated streets were opened up during this period and here the influence of Nash and Decimus Burton often lies with a light, but clearly discernible, hand. These Late Regency and Early Victorian years saw, in the area of the Parade, the creation of the fine, flowing curve of Lansdowne Crescent, Beauchamp Square, Clarendon Square as well as the villas of Portland Street and Warwick Street. To this period also belongs the development of the estate of Newbold Comyn which, in 1820, was bequeathed to his son by the Rev. Edward Willes. A large area of the estate was given over to building and, in course of time, gave rise to the spacious, elegant squares and terraces which were connected to the Parade by a road built through the estate from Holly Walk. Newbold Common itself, however – sometimes called Newbold Meadows – was not to be included in the development plans and the area was presented to the town to be preserved as an open space. It is now known as Jephson Gardens after one of the spa's most celebrated physicians, though there is a memorial obelisk to Willes in the grounds. The gardens face the Royal Pump Room, which has its own extensive grounds, and nearby is Victoria Park, the whole area making a wedge of open land that reaches into the very heart of the resort.

In the years after the visit of the Prince Regent Leamington was to enjoy the patronage of the rich and famous, including Dickens, Longfellow, the Duke of Wellington, Ruskin and Queen Victoria, whose statue now looks out on the Parade from before the pastiche Renaissance Town Hall. Its social life, however, never aspired to be on quite the same scale as that of Cheltenham and Leamington was always to be rather more of a serious health resort than a pleasure centre. It was, perhaps, this early concentration that has helped to preserve it into our own times as the leading health spa in England, many thousands of patients still annually attend the Pump Room for treatment under various specialists.

But, as was the case with Cheltenham, Leamington's spa functions long ago ceased to dominate the town. These had their last fling in the years immediately after 1844 when the railway arrived enabling the journey to London to be undertaken in just over four hours. For some years this assured the spa of a reasonably steady, if gradually declining, flow of custom. But, by the late 1850s, the decline had become so marked that Leamington, in common with similar towns, was beginning to turn its attentions to developing itself primarily as a residential centre.

By 1860 the position of the spa had become so perilous that the owner of the Pump Room announced his intention of disposing of the property for building development. Fortunately the announcement resulted in the formation of a new company which, taking over the rooms, effected improvements and were eventually responsible for them being operated by the local Board of Health. It was this 'municipalisation' of Leamington's major spa facility that was chiefly responsible for the town continuing as a spa into the present century.

While the popularity of Leamington and Cheltenham as health centres began to tail off in the 1840s and 1850s the northern spa of Harrogate was also in the doldrums. It had already experienced one bout of 'spa fever' which had culminated in the erection of its Royal Pump Room in 1842. But, unlike the Midland spas, it was destined to enjoy a revival which was ultimately to elevate it as England's leading spa town and finally to make it the national rival to the fashionable Continental spas such as Homburg, Marienbad and Carlsburg.

We have already observed that Harrogate's waters were first discovered in the late sixteenth century. Like Leamington, however, its evolution as a spa was to be a slow one. But it was greatly to benefit by its geographical location and, once having outstripped Knaresborough and Scarborough, it was able to claim, with some justification, that it was the only fashionable spa for the North. When, before the coming of the railways, it had reached a stage where Buxton, lying many miles to the south by jolting stage-coach, was its nearest rival, it had in effect achieved the position of having almost a captive clientele.

The earliest accounts of Harrogate's wells were published by Edmund Deane and Michael Stanhope in the early seventeenth century and from these it is clear that – despite

William Slingsby's so-called 'discovery' of the Teewit Well in 1571 – the wells in the Harrogate region at large had been used by local people for medicinal purposes for many years. As a result of these and subsequent publications – all extolling the various healing properties of the Harrogate waters – visitors from all over the North began arriving at the wells. But, as has been said earlier, because Harrogate was then two distinct small rural communities, known as High and Low Harrogate, neither having the facilities required by wealthy cure-takers, the visitors tended to centre their actual stay upon neighbouring Knaresborough.

Largely due to the presence of Knaresborough the development of Harrogate was very gradual – though, by 1700, there were three substantial inns on the edge of the moors at High Harrogate and a considerable number of lodging houses for visitors where mineral baths could be taken. Despite the popularity of the wells most of the visitors seemed, from their various accounts, to agree with Daniel Defoe that the smell of the Old Sulphur Well was 'foetid and nauseous'. Nonetheless, many made repeated visits.

One of present-day Harrogate's major features is not to be found amongst its buildings but in The Stray itself, the tract of well-tended parkland that girdles the centre of the town. In the 1770s it was proposed – at the onset of the second great enclosure movement in English history – to enclose the common land of the Forest of Knaresborough. But it was specifically stated that the land between the various wells should not be enclosed. To this particular piece of eighteenth-century legislation Harrogate owes one of its greatest attractions to visitors and residents alike.

In 1788 Harrogate acquired its first permanent theatre and, in 1793, a racecourse was laid out on part of The Stray. Lord Loughborough erected a high cupola over one of the wells – the St John Well – and planted a line of trees to make an attractive walk after the example of Skillicorne's Cheltenham Well Walk. In 1804 a second cupola arrived on the scene, this time erected over the Old Sulphur Well, and the following year saw the completion of the Promenade Room, now known as the Old Town Hall.

Harrogate emerged into the post-Napoleonic years as a spa

which had somehow managed to attract an extensive clientele but which still lacked, compared to the spas of the south, all but the most rudimentary facilities. But confidence was growing in the town. Its old dependency on nearby Knaresborough had been almost completely severed and a new class of enterprising well-owners were soon to project the spa forward into the first period of real expansion.

The first move in this expansion was modest enough with the erection of a pump-room over a newly discovered well near the Ripon road. It was owned by John Williams who now named it the Cheltenham Saline Well because a local medical authority considered that its waters resembled those of Cheltenham.

In 1832 Joseph Thackwray, the owner of the Crown Hotel, began to exploit springs discovered on land on the east side of the hotel, erecting a pump-room in the style of an Oriental pagoda and laying out gardens and pleasure grounds.

Owners of small hotels and lodging houses which were not able to offer the facilities of mineral baths on their premises were to be instrumental in opening the first public mineral baths in Harrogate in 1828. The Starbeck Baths were extended in the 1830s and in 1832 John Williams, of the Cheltenham Saline Well, opened public baths adjoining the Promenade Room. Not to be outdone, Joseph Thackwray built a larger bathing establishment in the gardens of his sulphur springs two years later. Thackwray's baths were later to be renamed the Montpellier.

In 1835 John Williams replaced the small pump-room at the Cheltenham Saline Well with a saloon fronted by a Classical portico. Named the Royal Promenade and Cheltenham Pump Room it was later to be rechristened as the Royal Spa Concert Room and to be mainly used for dancing and concerts. Behind the building a lake was created by damming a small river and the surrounding land laid out as an ornamental garden in which a band played on fine days. Over this period private building began to link up the two originally separate parts of Harrogate and, near to the Crown Hotel, Joseph Thackwray was to be responsible for the erection of a reading room and library, another indispensible element of the successful spa town.

In 1841 Harrogate came something near to possessing a town council when an Act of Parliament was obtained to set up a body to be known as the Harrogate Improvement Commissioners. These men were primarily interested in fostering the development of the spa and one of their first acts was to plan a new pump-room to be erected at the site of the old Sulphur Well. This was completed the following year to the design of a local architect, Isaac Shutt, in the shape of an octagonal building named the Royal Pump Room.

Judging from the history of most other English spa towns the date of the building of the Royal Pump Room would seem to have heralded the town's decline. But, unlike Cheltenham's Pittville Pavilion, the new Harrogate Royal Pump Room was to rank as far more than a memorial. Harrogate, at this period, held its own while visitors to the spas of the south and Midlands fell rapidly away. Just why Harrogate managed to weather the mid-Victorian years which spelt the end of so many English spas must remain something of a mystery. But, undoubtedly, its initial survival was due to the nearness of a prosperous middle class in the industrial towns of the North – especially in the West Riding – which had come to regard it equally as a resort and a spa. By the time that spa-going revived on the crest of the wave of the new science of hydropathy, Harrogate was sufficiently established for it to be able to enter the new European spa-league from the solid foundation of municipal enterprise.

In Cheltenham, however, it was to be a far different story. Here the decline of the Regency leisure-spa was to be positively hastened by the intervention of the puritanical and sabbatarian Dean Francis Close, who was also to be intimately associated with Cheltenham's mid-nineteenth century emergence as a school-town. Whatever his good points, however, and they were not altogether lacking, in relation to Cheltenham's spa life the influence of Francis Close can be described as nothing less than a blight.

Close arrived in Cheltenham in 1826, first as curate of Holy Trinity, later becoming rector of St Mary's. He was to wage a ceaseless war of social attrition against Colonel Berkeley, now created Earl FitzHardinge and Baron Segrave. It was a war of the new Victorian morality against what may be termed the somewhat loose ranks of Whig and post-Regency liberality and, although Berkeley was to remain a potent influence on Cheltenham life throughout the years of Close's ministry, it was a war whose victory ultimately went to the Evangelical cleric.

Close began his 'clean-up-Cheltenham' campaign with a sermon, later printed as a tract, against the recently established Cheltenham Races and its fringe, on-course amusements. He raised a furious storm of protest from the Berkeley faction and, although he was unsuccessful in seeing the closure of the Races, the character of its associated fair was to become increasingly sober.

Close also directed his displeasure toward the theatre and when, in May 1839, the Theatre Royal was burnt to the ground in a fire for which no cause could be found, the censorious minister probably attributed this to one of the more favourable acts of God.

His antipathy to the new railways – in which he was certainly not alone – was, in Cheltenham's case, a considerable influence in seeing that the new form of transport did not provide the town with a direct link to London until 1845. To some extent this was to contribute directly to the decline of the spa for many other spa centres were linked to London by rail and many of the other major cities long before this time and may, because of this, have attracted some of Cheltenham's former patrons.

By the late 1840s Close had so stamped his evangelical and reforming character upon Cheltenham that it was already earning for itself the image of the sober, puritanical and conservative town which was to be its most durable characteristic and which was to effectively erase all but the faintest image of the fashionable frivolity and license of the Regency bonanza.

Close, however, was to engage in other activities which were destined to bring to the town something more than the deadly fame of sober provincialism. From the early 1840s until he left the town to become Dean of Carlisle in 1856 he was to be closely involved in the development of local private education though, as was to be expected, his involvement was to have a marked Evangelical bias.

In 1841 he was to be one of the moving spirits behind the foundation of the Cheltenham Proprietory College – now Cheltenham College and the first public school to be founded in Victoria's reign. Its early years were far from smooth and under its first headmaster, the Rev Albert Phillips, conditions and teaching methods were so bad that there were frequent school riots and many parents withdrew their children. The school was first housed in two buildings in Bayshill Terrace moving to the present nucleus in 1843. But the school's disorders were not finally quelled until Phillips was removed three years later to be replaced by William Dobson who refused to push Close's evangelical dogma down the boys' reluctant throats.

It was to be another seven years before the founding of the college's sister institution, the 'proprietory college for the education of young ladies'. This went through the same type of disorder and disaster in its early years as the boys' school. But Close was less involved in its affairs than he had been with the earlier foundation, probably comforting himself with the thought that certain parallels of early indiscipline would probably lead to later, more acceptable, similarities, in that the well-educated young ladies from the new establishment would doubtless become fitting mates for the equally well-educated young gentlemen from Cheltenham College. After all, after the gruelling experience of a nineteenth-century English public-school education both sexes could be expected to emerge almost completely insensitive to anything, including each other.

In the mid-forties Close had turned his attention to education at the other end of the spectrum and had been active in establishing a number of infant schools in the town. His philosophy here seems to have owed a lot to St Ignatius Loyola – though such a parallel would probably have given Close a fit of apoplexy. His aim was to combat the propaganda machine of the Tractarians by popping as many Cheltenham children as he could into infant schools and vaccinating them with Evangelicanism against the new disease. The infant schools naturally needed teachers and Close provided for this by the establishment of St Paul's Teacher Training College in 1849. Later he was instrumental in seeing a women's training college, St Mary's, established in St George's Place.

This one-man Department of Education was not to stop here. In 1848 he turned his attention to Pate's Grammar School – the oldest school in the town. It was endowed through Corpus Christ College, Oxford – but was falling into neglect. At the head of the 'Vestry Committee of resolute men' Close had the old school closed, later to be reopened with an additional classroom, a new teaching scheme and a new Headmaster of Evangelical persuasion.

By the time Close left for Carlisle in 1856 Cheltenham's new role was largely established. Despite the presence of Colonel Berkeley – who was to die the following year after a fall in the hunting field – it was no longer even an echo of its former Regency self. Truly Close could never have claimed that he had been supported by everyone – but he had certainly been supported by enough. Over the three decades of his ministry Cheltenham had seen its local emphasis shift from the Classical pump-rooms to the new Victorian Gothic churches which had sprouted up all over the town – from the headiness of Regency merrymaking to the soberness of the new Victorian morality. After the death of Colonel Berkeley it was a town in which Queen Victoria would have positively enjoyed not being "amused".

Leamington passed through a similar change of style over these years – but without the dominating influence of a man such as Francis Close. In fact, although Leamington was also affected by the new Victorian 'morality', its change from spa to residential centre was more obviously due to economic pressures. Its large houses, which had once held the aristocracy – who now preferred to take their pleasures at the less-inhibited Continental resorts – were largely to be taken by the retired builders of empire, the civil servants and half-pay officers who had long dreamed of one day returning to spend their last years 'at home'. They, and their successors, were to form a substantial part of Leamington's population well into the middle years of the present century.

But, although the large houses may have been full of gouty Indian army colonels, the town had to expand to accommodate all who wished to settle there. From 1846 until around the turn of the century the town's population rose by approximately a thousand each year – quite a large figure when it is considered that, as the town's population was biased toward the retired, the birthrate was amongst the lowest in the country. In fact, together with nearby Kenilworth and Warwick, Leamington was to develop as something of a residential and predominantly middle-class redoubt lying just to the south of the sprawl of the industrial Midlands. As is the case with Cheltenham, this bias has begun to weaken in more recent years.

Although the spa trade continued to enjoy a fitful existence it was no longer associated with the ebullient leisure activities which had characterised it in the days of the Regency. The beaux and rakes had long departed to be replaced by sufferers whose maladies had not been primarily caused by dissipation. Although entertainment, of a modest and relatively unobtrusive kind, was still offered at the Royal Pump Room, Leamington was now an earnest rather than a frivolous place.

But it was realised that the town still retained all the trappings of an inland resort and attempts were made to capitalise upon them. The world's first lawn-tennis club was to be founded in the town in 1872 and pointed the way for things to come. Over the next few years Leamington made a bid – with some success – to popularise itself as a sports' town – though croquet, for which it was to gain something of a national reputation, may not exactly be described as a passion which has lasted into present times. Today Leamington is still often chosen as the venue for the Amateur Athletics Association's events.

Shopkeepers and hoteliers still endeavoured to attract the visitor – but not to visit the mineral baths. Leamington was now seen as the gateway to the Shakespeare country, with Warwick and Kenilworth castles thrown in as a bonus. Stratford was soon to get its first Memorial Theatre and was already becoming a popular place, but it was not, and still could not claim to be, a shopping centre that could hope to rival Leamington and the spa-town's hotels easily outstripped those of their country cousin.

It was thus that Leamington entered the twentieth century, a town with a three-part function as residential centre, a medicinal-spa in the strictest sense of that term and as a recreational centre devoted, on the one hand, to sporting attractions and, on the other, to the encouragement of local tourism. All these functions have been retained and expanded into our own times and it seems a pity that so many other spa-towns failed to achieve this sort of balance which, in many cases was so essential to their survival.

Whilst Cheltenham, at least outwardly, was developing into a stronghold of Puritan reaction and Leamington was coming peacefully to terms with changed times, Harrogate was perched on the edge of England's last major spa convulsion. But, for a decade or more, the town was content to totter on the brink of its coming fame while the chaotic problems of its local government were being sorted out. At this time most of the spa's development was being undertaken by private enterprise – ambitious schemes were launched but generally came to grief after two or three years. In 1871 the Harrogate Improvement Commissioners took a hand in the game, rebuilding the Victoria Baths as the New Victoria Baths with a suite of eighteen baths. But it was private enterprise which, in 1878, showed the way Harrogate was to go over the next three decades. In this year the Swan Hotel was taken over by the Harrogate Hydropathic Company and converted into a fully-fledged hydro on the vigorously spartan pattern which had earlier met with such success at places such as Malvern and Matlock.

Things were to be greatly speeded up when Harrogate became a municipal borough in 1884 – for more money was now available for the council to take the initiative in developing the spa. Over the next few years the expansion of the spa was to be almost entirely a municipal enterprise, private development largely confining itself to the provision of sumptuous hotels and a rash of private schools. In fact

Harrogate, in these years, came to possess quite as many schools as Cheltenham – but this was almost the only similarity. Cheltenham, as a spa, was dying, if not yet completely dead. Harrogate, on the other hand, was thriving and looked forward to an even more expansive future.

By 1886 the new council was beginning to gain confidence and initiated various improvements to the New Victoria Baths. The land now known as Valley Gardens was also bought by the council at this time and laid out as a recreation area. Two years later the council was to acquire the Montpellier complex from George Dawson – who had bought it in 1884 and had added a skating-rink – with the original intention of extending the baths to form the nucleus of a spa which could complete on an equal footing with those of the Continent.

Before the work was begun a fact-finding mission was sent to some of the major European spas to study the latest examples of spa architecture and facilities. When it returned, however, the council was already moving away from its original intention to develop the existing Montpellier toward the much more radical idea of pulling down the old buildings and constructing an entirely new centre. For the next few years little was done – largely due to the problem of raising capital. But, as Harrogate's rateable value increased so did its borrowing powers, and in 1893 the council felt in a strong enough position to give the go-ahead for what was to be known as the Royal Baths.

The Royal Baths were opened in 1897 containing four suites of baths with a central hall where there were provided a variety of waters. The Baths included the glass-roofed Winter Gardens which were intended to double as a promenade room for those using the baths and also to function as a concert room. When, in 1900, the council acquired the Starsbeck Baths and the Prince of Wales Baths, their waters were also piped to the Royal Baths to supplement its facilities.

The building of the Royal Baths had not entailed the demolition of the old Montpellier Baths, as had originally been envisaged, and these were now to be converted into peat baths, a brine bath being added in 1903. The Royal Baths

were a successful attempt to rival the baths of the great
European spas – of which Harrogate was now undoubtably
one – and in all, more than forty different types of mineral
baths were available.

Harrogate was soon to turn its attention to provisions for
entertainment. The number of visitors who came to the resort
for general recreation rather than specifically to take the
waters far outweighed those who made serious use of the
Royal Baths. Various private theatres and halls made some
attempt to provide entertainment for visitors during the latter
years of the nineteenth century, the Town Hall Theatre – once
the Old Promenade Rooms – possibly being the most
successful. Various touring shows appeared at the New
Victoria Hall in James Street, including the Christy Minstrels.
But this theatre had difficulty in paying its way and went out
of business in 1892. In 1900 a consortium of local businessmen
provided the spa with an altogether more sumptuous building
in the form of the Grand Opera House which, besides music,
also offered drama, with Sarah Bernhardt making more than
one visit there.

The council was to take a hand in 1896 when it bought the
Spa Rooms Baths. Although it was to meet with much
opposition from the local ratepayers the council determined to
go ahead and erect a 'Kursaal' on the site – this building being
renamed The Royal Hall in 1914, a name it has retained to
the present day. The Kursaal included a theatre and went a
long way to rounding off Harrogate as the British zenith of the
spa experience.

The town was now catering very much for a middle-class
clientele, though with a generous sprinkling of the aristocracy
thrown in. In its Edwardian hey-day much of London society
moved north to the spa – and it was, perhaps, the fact that
they had to move to it, just as to Carlsbad or Homburg, that
made Harrogate so popular. The spa was also attracting
foreign royalty – the final stamp of establishment approval.

Harrogate was now attempting to build its reputation
around its claims to exclusiveness. A few years earlier this
had, in 1893, led to the borough seeking to secure an Act of
Parliament whereby it bought the rights of pasture on the

Stray from the freeholders. Affairs on the Stray had been giving cause for some alarm for many years, particularly in the light of Harrogate's attempt to assert itself as the most exclusive resort in England. In the words of one alderman, the Act of 1893 ensured "that there would be no circuses, no wild beast shows, no niggers holding their entertainments within seventy-five yards of any house".

Harrogate also did its best to discourage day-trippers and Sunday excursionists and local pulpits were often the platforms for sombre oratory that held that no good could come of working-class hordes disturbing the peace by pushing and elbowing their way through Valley Gardens. But this was hardly said in the spirit of Francis Close's 'new Victorian morality'. In Harrogate such sentiments were usually drawn from the well of rampant class-consciousness that underlay the latter years of Victoria's reign.

Harrogate was still expanding. In 1900 two of its largest hotels, The Grand and The Majestic were completed and it was soon being said that the Royal Baths were becoming so overcrowded that they could no longer cope with the number of bathers wishing to use them at the height of the season. Various plans for extensions were suggested, but were not made though, in 1914, the council took over Harlow Carr Baths in an attempt to cater for the growing numbers. The year before the spa had attracted more than 75,000 visitors and, though there were still misgivings on the part of some local ratepayers as to the amount of money their council had been spending, the general financial position of the spa was quite good. Given the enormous amount of money that had been spent, the spa institutions were managing to show a yearly surplus after all capital expenditure had been met. The trend pointed to a future of ever increasing prosperity. But it was now 1914 and Harrogate, so tied up with the buoyancy of the Edwardian era, was soon to all-but-disintegrate under the impact of changing times.

While Harrogate had been aspiring to – and reaching – heights of grandeur, Cheltenham had been content to aim for minor glories. To some extent it had, by the 1890s, broken free from the atmosphere of restraint once imposed by Francis

Close. Close had died in 1882 and he was to be commemorated, four years later, by the building of the Dean Close Memorial School on the Shelbourne Road, a mile and a half from the town centre. But, though Close was dead and his influence largely dispersed, Cheltenham's new air of liberation was to come too late to rescue it as a spa.

Nevertheless, brave attempts were to be made. The glass-roofed structure of the Winter Gardens was opened on the site before the Queen's Hotel, now known as the Imperial Gardens. Balls and concerts were held here, as well as at the Assembly Rooms and, in 1891, Cheltenham at last gained a theatre to replace the old Theatre Royal, in the Opera House which was to see performances by most of the famous players of the day. Clinging desperately to the hope that Cheltenham' could somehow emulate the success of Harrogate the council bought the Pittville Pump Room and, in 1893, the Montpellier Gardens, announcing that it intended to develop both "on lines similar to those adopted at Continental resorts".

Municipal efforts to revive the flagging fortunes of the spa were of little avail. True enough, some visitors did again come to Cheltenham, attending the Winter Garden concerts and strolling along the Promenade. But this could not mask the fact that, behind its Regency facades, Cheltenham was really a town in decay. In 1900 the Assembly Rooms were to be demolished to make way for a branch of Lloyd's Bank and, in the following year, the final bout of municipal enterprise in relation to the spa saw the opening of the new 'Renaissance-style' Town Hall where balls and concerts could now take place and which offered a wide variety of Cheltenham's waters to those who cared to take them. Not many did.

Hoteliers and shopkeepers had long ago ceased to stress that Cheltenham was a spa-town. Instead they saw its future in attracting them by publicising Cheltenham as a 'Garden Town' and as 'The Centre for the Cotswolds' – the Wordsworthian passion for the picturesque was still sending the urban English into the countryside in search of both beauty and relaxation. But even this attempted change of direction was scarcely enough to save the resort. The reputation the town had acquired during its 'Close years' still

clung and popular opinion outside the town seems to have
been that the place was a fossil, dead, but by some miracle still
on its feet. Hotels closed down and many of the large houses
were empty or converted into flats. With a dwindling number
of visitors unemployment became an acute local problem for,
apart from the local brewery, there was hardly any industry in
the town. Poverty, in a more general sense, was not confined
to the town's poorer quarters, and behind many a genteel
façade it was more than a struggle to maintain the
appearances which residence in middle-class Cheltenham
implied.

Only the town's schools could be said to be doing really well.
New ones were opened in the early 1900s and, under Dorothea
Beale, its first head, the Ladies' College had continued to
expand almost from the first moment of its foundation.

But, the schools apart, it was a rather dismal Cheltenham
that arrived at the tumultuous year of 1914 – a town which
had lost its way and which had no idea where to go. It was the
war which was to point the way, for the arrival of new industry
on its outskirts was a foretaste of things to come. Subsequently
it was destined to develop both as a residential centre and,
with increasing emphasis, as a dormitory town for the new
industry to the south.

Of the English spas to survive into 1914 it was Harrogate
alone which had jumped national boundaries to enter the
nineteenth century European rather than the English spa
tradition. In its social style, its considerable assembly of
public – yet at the same time exclusive – buildings, by its vast
and calculated municipal interest in various aspects of spa
promotion, with its ultimate attraction of royalty and the
nobility in general, even in its obvious aping of German
models in the naming of the Kuursall and its sending of civic
architects to study the buildings of Continental spas, it made a
bid to be taken seriously as a European rather than a purely
English social centre. In later years even Neville Chamberlain
was to recuperate here.

Buxton and Llandrindod tried to emulate it – but never
quite succeeded. Cheltenham made a hollow effort to copy its
style – but was both too late and too meagre in its civic

investment. Bath and Tunbridge slumbered and, as spas, developed no more. After the Great War even Harrogate's massive pretensions lay in tatters.

4

The Victorian Spas

The Victorian spas differed from most of their predecessors in a number of things, but chiefly in the fact that almost everywhere, the health aspect of the spa resort was to be put very much before its pleasure aspect. In fact, while most of the major earlier centres survived, in one way or another, into this period, their survival was, to a considerable extent, dependent upon them supplementing their original provisions with those now popularised by the newer health centres.

Of the new centres it was Malvern which was to most clearly indicate the direction in which both the new and existing spas were now headed. Malvern's waters had been known since at least the middle ages when St Anne's Well had acquired a reputation for curing eye complaints. There was a chalybeate spring – but Malvern's waters were to be chiefly valued for their purity. However, for many years, their reputation was only a local one and they were to be amongst the few in the country which were *not* to receive a visit from that enthusiastic well-seeker Celia Fiennes.

Although local physicians were aware of the waters' curative properties it was largely the efforts of one man, Dr John Wall, who was first to bring them to more than local notice. Wall was one of those eighteenth-century men of many parts. Born at Powick in 1708 he was later a pupil at Leigh School, attended Merton College, Oxford and eventually returned to set up medical practice in Worcester. He was something of an artist and a considerable chemist, becoming one of the founders of the Worcester Tonquin Manufactory, later to become known, in the nineteenth century, as the Royal Worcester Porcelain Company. He was a founder member and physician of the Worcester Infirmary and it was this interest that seems to have first led him towards Malvern's wells. Poor patients were advised to seek out the waters in the small village beneath the hills and those who were unable to travel were to be provided with water bottled at the wells.

The Malvern waters were already drawing a small, but fashionable patronage, before John Wall took an active interest in them. But the visitors came mostly as an overflow from nearby Cheltenham – presumably to be cured from an excess of curing there. Lodging consisted of one house, Abbey House, which could accommodate only fifteen visitors – any more than this having to take their chance at local farms. Wall was later to be responsible for organising a committee of Worcester gentry to improve Malvern's walks and accommodation. But, in 1774, he retired from practice, moved to Bath and died there two years later. He had been so closely associated with the centre that it suffered a temporary lapse in popularity from which it did not begin to recover until his son, Martin, collated his father's 'Malvern' writings and reissued them in one volume.

For the next two or three decades Malvern prospered in a modest way, chiefly due to the efforts of Worcester-based physicians of whom Dr James Johnson and Dr Wilson Phillips were the most influential. Visitors began to come in such numbers that the earlier three month season was, by the 1830s, extended to run from March to December.

Malvern was now functioning as a minor spa, offering, apart from its waters, rest and relaxation in a relatively peaceful environment. The social round was hardly a taxing one and, in general, Malvern's visitors were genuinely in need of a therapeutic holiday. It was, at all events, scarcely the place for the beaux and rakes who had characterised the life of the earlier spas.

The centre of local popularity was to shift from Malvern Wells to Great Malvern when both the Royal Library and the public Baths were built opposite the Unicorn Hotel. The Library, built in late-Classical style by John Deykes, contained, apart from the library itself, a music room, bazaar, reading room and a billiards room. The Baths, also built by John Deykes, consisted of a pump-room and a suite of baths offering various combinations of the local waters.

At the same time as this new centre was being created the local vicar, the Rev Henry Card, was bending his efforts toward the restoration of the ancient Priory while Mary, Countess Harcourt, was providing the money for laying out a series of hill-walks to show her appreciation for the benefits the spa had bestowed upon her health. In less refined style, horse-racing was initiated as an additional attraction which brought in people from all over the surrounding area as well as from Malvern itself. Pugilistic contests were also staged on nearby Welland Common though the bloody spectacles created by these were, perhaps, hardly likely to assist the delicate spa-goers toward recovery.

The activities of the spa were, however, destined to be revolutionised by the arrival in 1842 first of Dr James Wilson and secondly of Dr James Manby Gully. Both had received sound, conventional medical training but had tired of the application of orthodox medicine which, in many cases, they considered to be positively harmful to their patients. Accordingly Wilson had spent several months in Silesia at the establishment of Vincenz Priestnitz, the pioneer of the 'water-cure'. He had returned to England determined to set up a similar establishment and fired Gully, whom he had known professionally for some time previously, with the same enthusiasm. Both men decided that Malvern, with its hills, pure water and pure air was the best available English counterpart to Priestnitz's Graffenburg.

With Wilson leasing the Crown Hotel, rechristening it 'Graffenburg House' and Gully taking Tudor House for men and Holyrood House for women, Malvern was to be launched on its career as a hydropathic centre. The efforts of the two hydropaths aroused fervent hostility from local doctors – but Wilson and Gully were to prove generally successful and many cures were to be attributed to their treatments. In part much of the opposition must be ranked as medical sour grapes, for both the hydropaths attracted the patients of local medical men and, in more cases than not, seem to have succeeded where their more conventional colleagues had failed. Wilson succeeded to such a degree that he was able to move into Priestnitz House in 1845 – a vastly more commodious and generously equipped building than the Crown.

For some years the two doctors had the field largely to themselves, though Gully was to emerge as the more fashionable of the two, largely, perhaps, because Wilson was to acquire the reputation of being something of a martinet and people tended to favour Gully's more urbane approach to wet-sheeting, cold douching, wet-packs and the rest of the hydropathic timetable.

In course of time a rift developed between the two former friends and it was from about this time that other doctors began to wend their way toward Malvern to benefit financially from the effects of the water-cure. Hydropathic establishments mushroomed, some complete with newer curative methods including electropathy and, in the case of Dr Grindrod, the compressed-air bath.

Malvern was now more freely accessible, for in 1861, the railway finally arrived at the town. For some years afterwards Malvern's hydros thrived as they were never to thrive again. But events were to prove them a passing phase. The rise of the Continental spas and of more sophisticated medical methods led to scorn and ridicule being heaped on hydropaths in general. A spate of prosecutions alleging that individual hydropaths had in fact murdered their patients by the water-cure can hardly be said to have elevated the profession.

As Malvern's hydropaths retired or died there were few willing to carry on their dwindling businesses – many of the buildings being converted either as hotels or schools. By 1900 only Priestnitz House was still in business and this now under the name of the County Hydropathy – for Priestnitz and Graffenburg would have meant very little to those who now used it. It was now run by a Dr J.N.F. Fergusson who was achieving modest success. But, in 1905, the establishment was forced to close following an outbreak of typhoid fever. Fergusson was ruined and Malvern, as a spa and hydropathic centre, was dead. It was, indeed, to live on, for a number of years, as a popular inland resort – but its attractions were now of the picturesque variety, walks on the hills, views from the

Beacon, good meals in the hotels, leisurely entertainment at the Winter Gardens. Its future development – as indeed some of its past development had already been – was to be as a school-town and residential centre.

The nearby resort of Tenbury Wells was to have a far more modest life. Its saline wells were not discovered until 1839 when efforts were being made to tap a new water supply. In later years a pump-room was to be erected which was supposed to have resembled an Oriental pagoda; it was a supposition that fell far short of realisation. The Pump Room is unusual in that it was partially built in sheet-metal which is now rusting away in the Worcestershire rains and is in a sad state of dilapidation. Plans have been suggested to preserve the building but nothing has been done. No doubt it will be readily mourned once it has gone.

Tenbury had only the slimmest of chances of ever making it as a big-time spa. Its waters were discovered when it was still an over-night stopping place for North Wales – London coaches and this was enough to provide it with a modest trickle of visitors. They were hardly sufficient to justify any expansion and Tenbury's spa functions were to be essentially a graft onto a rural market-town. Accommodation was limited to existing inns, namely the King's Head and the Royal Oak, although the town was subsequently to sprout a few large houses.

By the time the railway reached Tenbury its reputation was not that of a spa but, as we have already observed in relation to nearby Malvern, that of a picturesque resort. The Pump Room continued to nourish a small number of visitors in this peaceful town upon the Teme. However, it probably receives far more visitors in this age of the motor-car than it ever did when it first bid to enter the ranks of the spas. It is doubtful, though, if any of them visit the Pump Room pagoda which, tucked away behind the main street and rusting through the years, is no longer a sight which many would wish to see.

Far the most successful of the three Victorian spa towns to be found in Worcestershire was Droitwich. Its salt was known to the Romans who extracted it here for use all over Britain and for export to the northern provinces of their empire.

Whether they erected public baths at Droitwich is not known. But it is rather doubtful, for Roman Droitwich seems to have been almost exclusively an industrial centre with few Romano-Celtic tycoons about who wished to wash away the effects of over-indulgent living.

As the centre of the salt-trade it greatly pre-dated the Roman occupation, for the salt ways leading to the south and west existed long before the Romans came. They were to be used long after the Romans left and Wyche was the salt capital of England throughout Anglo Saxon and medieval times – producing a commodity which was highly valued in a society that would have had a meatless winter if it had not been for salting.

Salt continued to be produced in the town until the early 1920s – but long before then Droitwich had basically changed its function from industrial centre to spa. The change was predominantly due to the efforts of John Corbett, 'The Salt King', who had made borings outside the old town which, coupled with the introduction of new extracting techniques, meant that both a better quality and greater quantity of brine could be extracted at his new works at Stoke Prior. Much of Corbett's business now moved from the ancient centre to the new site, a process that was speeded up when Corbett's company became amalgamated with the Salt Union – which had a virtual monopoly of salt manufacture in England.

Having deprived Droitwich of most of its old industry. John Corbett was moved to create another to take its place. The town's potential as a spa came to light quite by chance in 1832. Cholera had broken out in the town and local doctors were urging the wealthy – their only customers in those generally tight-belted days – to seek a remedy in taking frequent hot baths. This piece of advice filtered down to the salt workers and their families, who were no less immune from the epidemic and who could not even afford the luxury of cold baths let alone hot ones. They solved the problem by jumping into the warm brine vats and the effects of this were so impressive in warding off the disease that the wealthy were soon taking hot brine baths of their own.

Seeing the results of this treatment local doctors were not

slow off the mark. Various ailments were treated with hot brine baths and it was found to be especially effective in treating rheumatic disorders. A company was floated and in 1840 the Royal Baths were opened to cater for the growing inflow of invalid visitors.

It was in somewhat later years that John Corbett took a hand in Droitwich's spa development. He was largely responsible for grafting a completely new town onto the old. On the high ground above the River Salwarpe Corbett was the influence behind the creation of broad roads, new hotels, Salter's Hall – later to be converted into a cinema – and of the St Andrew's Brine Baths. A park was provided where an orchestra played in season and the larger hotels had their own gardens, tennis and croquet courts. In fact, Corbett provided Droitwich with all the trappings of a serious health resort. His own house, Chateau Impney, built in French style for his Parisian wife, is now also a hotel and conference centre.

Droitwich's spa activities survived until recent years when, because the facilities offered by the St Andrew's Brine Baths could now be duplicated by a hospital, the National Health Service backing for them was withdrawn. The salt content of the brine baths was so high that it was not difficult for patients, if not actually to walk upon the waters, then certainly to float upon them and take tea while doing so. The town, however, still exists as a spa. It retains its open-air lido – which advertises 'sea bathing' – and its hotels still do a good trade.

Since the mid-1930s – with considerable acceleration in more recent years – Droitwich has been going the same way as modern Cheltenham with the attraction of new industries and their consequent working population. Within this new outer belt there still remains much of the older town, the spa creation and the later residential development of the late Victorian and Edwardian years.

In the years of Droitwich's budding spa enterprise there was to grow another Midland spa far away from the Worcestershire Plain but sharing a local geography that shared many similarities with Malvern. This was Shropshire's Church Stretton, tucked close into the slopes of the Long

Mynd and lying in the valley between it and neighbouring
Caer Caradoc. Like Malvern its waters were noted for their
purity and had a local reputation in the eighteenth century.
But Church Stretton's development as a spa belongs almost
exclusively to the mid-nineteenth century.

It was then that the railway reached the town, providing a
link to Shrewsbury and North Wales and, at the same time, to
South Wales and the West. From this time dates the main
thoroughfare of the spa, Sandford Avenue, lying between the
new railway station and the old village centre of church and
market square.

But, although the village functioned as a spa, its waters
were never its chief attraction. Earlier than Malvern it realised
that its future lay in stressing its qualities as a 'rest-centre'
though the rest-cure would have been of a rather strenuous
kind. Walks could be taken over the Mynd or Caer Caradoc or
along some of the valleys such as Callow Hollow or
Cardingmill. So much was this aspect of Church Stretton
emphasized that the resort was never to possess a pump room,
only an ornate public drinking fountain. After a day spent
struggling over the hills, teetotallers at least, probably
welcomed this minimal form of refreshment.

It was to develop quickly as a resort for the retired and was
much favoured for its reputedly mild climate – though it
certainly has more than its fair share of rain. Its hotels still
function well 'in season', though the town is now a touring
centre rather than a spa, also attracting parties of geological
students who come to study the peculiar rock formations of
the nearby hills. Cardingmill Valley has been turned into a
fully fledged 'tourist trap' for visitors from the Midland towns,
complete with 'Alpine' restaurant, self service cafeteria and
ice-cream and hot-dog stands. It may be a fine day out for the
kids, who can run over the heather and splash about in the
small streams but, personally, the valley nowadays seems
something to be well out of. There is a Music and Arts Festival
promoted by the local Arts Association, most of the events
taking place in the town's relatively new secondary school –
this part of Shropshire has yet to go comprehensive and
grammar school pupils have to travel daily either to
Shrewsbury or Ludlow.

An eighteenth-century print of Bath by Thomas Loggon

The Pantiles at Tunbridge Wells in 1699

(left) Beau Nash (right) Beau Brummel

The Royal Crescent, Bath

The Roman Bath and Abbey, Bath

The Pump Room, Bath

The Pump Room at Bath, 1798, by Rowlandson

"It shocks me to see them look paler than ashes,
And as dead in the eye as the bust of Nash is,
Who the evening before were so blooming and plump,
I'm grieved to the heart when I go to the pump."

A nineteenth-century satirical drawing of the votaries of hydropathy

The Cross Bath, Bath, 1738, by L. Fayram

Fountains in the Promenade, Cheltenham

The Rotunda, formerly part of the Montpellier spa, Cheltenham

The Raven Hotel, Droitwich, remodelled by Corbett *c.* 1830

Over the border in Radnorshire, Llandrindod Wells is one of the few spas that still remains in active business. Llandrindod Wells, which was already doing quite well for itself, really blossomed when the railway arrived in 1866. Houses and hotels proliferated as a direct result and, although its late Victorian development was along somewhat different lines, in many ways it can be compared to the growth of Harrogate at roughly the same time.

It has been estimated that somewhere in the region of 90,000 people were visiting the spa annually by the close of the century. Llandrindod now boasted two assembly rooms, a Pavilion and Pump Room, broad paved streets, more than a dozen hotels and innumerable small guest-houses. It had a common, a lake, a wide area of parkland at its centre and, above all, waters that were claimed to be the equal of any to be found in Europe. There were thirty mineral wells providing, amongst others, saline, chalybeate and sulphur.

Industrial development has been sparse in this region – what there has been seeming to be largely confined to Montgomeryshire's Newtown – and Llandrindod has wisely concentrated on making itself an inland holiday centre. The spa treatment can still be had here – not through the National Health Service, however, but privately. But most people come for the clear air, the nearby countryside, the fishing, golf and general restfulness of a place that has managed to fuse the past elegance of the spa with the more energetic holiday favoured by those wishing to get away from the sedentary and tedious and, for a few days, to eschew the confines of the motor-car.

Just across the Breconshire border is Builth Wells, which cannot be said to have survived as well into the twentieth century as Llandrindod – if only because there was so much less to survive anyway. Builth waters had a local reputation in the eighteenth century when the Park Wells, some little way out of the town, had a considerable popularity amongst the local gentry. A promenade was constructed leading down from the bridge toward the wells which, however, were to lose some of their devotees when Lady Hester Stanhope settled at Glan Irfon and brought importance to the hitherto rather neglected Glana Wells.

Builth's nineteenth-century development – or lack of it –

suffered very much by the exploitation of the springs at Llandrindrod, so that, by the mid-nineteenth century, it was already something of a backwater, once more dominantly pursuing life as a small market-town.

Nowadays its visitors are chiefly of the fly-fishing fraternity with a sprinkling of those who fancy rural scenery for its own sake and the added reality of seclusion.

Far away in Westmorland arose another spa which was to experience much the same sort of fate as befell Builth Wells. This was Gilsland Spa which, in its brief hey-day, was the scene of the meeting of Sir Walter Scott and the girl he was later to marry and take to Abbotsford, Charlotte Carpenter. It was, in fact, a resort greatly patronised by the Border gentry and was later to form the basis of one of Scott's less-successful novels *St Ronan's Well*.

There were a number of other spas in the area, including Hexham and Shap Spa, but it was Gilsland which bid to be the most fashionable. It was of Gilsland that it was sometimes claimed that its waters had dried up when a speculating landlord built a house over the original well-head, thus robbing the local poor of their free 'cure-all'. But this was in the days before 'polite society' moved into the town. At their advent the waters seem to have been flowing freely enough. Although, because of its relative inaccessibility, Gilsland never stood much chance of taking off into the major spa-league, it successfully sprouted a Spa Hotel and a small pavilion near the well-head Pump Room. Today Gilsland retains no particular spa or resort tradition and has become just one more village visited by those touring the Lake District or the Border Country.

The rise of Buxton in Victorian times was something altogether more grand. It was often to be called 'The Bath of the North' or 'The Harrogate of the Midlands', but it owed little to either and was a spa of unusual individuality. Nearby Matlock was also to flourish during this period – but the development of the two centres was quite distinct.

Buxton had a tradition of thermal bathing going back, at least, to Roman times though, as in the case of Bath, this had lapsed for some centuries following the Roman withdrawal. But Buxton was a considerably developed spa by the end of the eighteenth century and was to grow so that it was, together with Llandrindrod Wells, to be one of the two spas which, in Victorian times, could most hope to mount a real challenge to the pre-eminence of Harrogate.

During the middle ages its main well, St Anne's, had a reputation for all manner of cures and a storehouse of abandoned crutches was at one time kept nearby. During the Reformation Thomas Cromwell had the crutches removed and the well was closed. However, it was soon in business again, for during the reign of Elizabeth I, George Talbot, Earl of Shrewsbury, allowed his ailing captive Mary, Queen of Scots, to visit the well a number of times. The fame of the waters were sufficient for them to merit a visit from Celia Fiennes toward the end of the seventeenth century.

The subsequent development of Buxton owed much to the Dukes of Devonshire. Both the well and bath were sited in the grounds of Buxton Hall which was in the ownership of the Cavendish Dukes and, in 1780, the fifth Duke gave directions for the building of the Crescent on the site of the former Roman Baths. Designed by the Yorkshireman John Carr, the Crescent was to remain as the main architectural glory of Buxton with its curve extending to 200 feet. In front of it stood St Anne's Well, within the eastern wing were the Hot Baths and at the end of the western wing were the Natural Baths. The Crescent was completed in 1784 and within the next decade the Duke was also responsible for the creation of the wide carriageway of Duke's Drive and the Great Stables summounted by an enormous dome – the latter now being the Royal Devonshire Hospital. Other buildings were to grow up near the Crescent and Buxton was well on the way to becoming a fashionable resort. By the end of the Regency period it possessed all the trappings of a successful spa now having its Pump Room, Broad Walk and a colonnade of fashionable shops as well as the Quadrant which now supplemented the Crescent.

The public bathing at Buxton's baths, however, seems to have offended some of its more fastidious visitors and a number of the leading hotels began to provide baths of their own.

But, despite its extensive facilities, Buxton was not destined to become a truly leading spa until the arrival of the railway coupled with the popular enthusiasm for the romantic notions of the outdoor life which had been popularised by the Lake poets and other writers who revered the rugged and 'Gothic' grand of Britain's wilder places. This new movement was to last throughout the nineteenth century and, away from Buxton, was to have George Borrow opening up the wonders of 'Wild Wales' as well as Byron declaring that the scenery of Derbyshire could bear comparison with any to be found in Switzerland or Germany.

The revolt from the Greek- and Roman-derived culture was well under way and, while it was certainly to exercise an adverse effect on spas such as Cheltenham and Bath, Buxton was ideally situated to profit from it. Rugged scenery was all right in itself, but it was greatly enhanced if there was a fashionable centre near at hand. Buxton, at the gateway to the 'High Peak', was able to capitalise on both its attractive position and on its waters. Visitors seeking to while away their days of leisure came for the scenery and amenities whilst those in search of the health-cure were adequately catered for as Buxton began to develop into a serious health spa. Its waters were said to resemble those of some of the leading French watering-places and various establishments were soon offering some of the newer cures such as the Vichy massage. As was the case with Malvern and Harrogate, bathing was to become only the most basic means of taking 'the cure' and, by the beginning of the twentieth century, Buxton's health establishments were offering vapour baths, compressed-air baths and emanations. The latter were the bathing in radioactive waters, which Buxton now claimed to have, and the inhaling of radioactive air which, as the town claimed to be covered in the element, was not difficult to do – though, of course, it was necessary to travel to Buxton to do it.

The town now sported a glass and iron-supported pavilion built by Sir Joseph Paxton, the designer of the Crystal Palace, in 1871, together with an Opera House, a spacious park and the enormous Palace Hotel. It was perfectly equipped to compete with Harrogate which it did with some success, although it never really tapped the social cream from the northern resort.

Buxton is still a leading member of the British Spas Federation, though nowadays its waters are hardly its major appeal. Like so many others it has become a sports and conference centre, while its hotels maintain a good seasonal holiday trade. Buxton winters can be particularly attractive as the resort now caters for skiing, tobogganing and curling. In summer there is the Well-Dressing Week and the town is now bending its attention toward promoting itself as an inland holiday resort with a multitude of exhibitions, good shopping facilities and as the entrance to the Peak District National Park.

Nearby Matlock was in and out of the spa business with the space of just over a century. Buxton, naturally, saw it come and go. In the late eighteenth century it possessed thermal baths and an assembly room – but it was too inaccessible really to attract many visitors. As the nearby roads were improved, largely due to the efforts of Richard Arkwright – whose cotton mill, the first mechanised textile factory in the world, was at nearby Cromford – the number of visitors increased. But it was not until the coming of the Midland Railway in 1849 and the intervention of John Smedley that Matlock really made its entrance into the eminence of spa promotion.

John Smedley was a local textile manufacturer who had made a small fortune, followed this by a bout of fashionable licence and dissipation and then decided to take himself to Europe on the Grand Tour. As a result of the latter two occupations he was soon to be reduced to a state of exhaustion and debility and came to a decision to end it all. His wife, however, persuaded him to try hydropathy as a last resort and Smedley was packed off to Ben Rhydding in Yorkshire, a hydropathic establishment of the strictest disciplines. Here, aided by a mixture of cold sheets and wet douches, Smedley was to undergo not only a conversion to hydropathy but a spiritual conversion too. Arriving back in Matlock he confidently announced that he was a new man – the change must have been quite remarkable for his wife now suffered a similar conversion in sympathy.

At first John Smedley was content to institute a scheme whereby his workers were smothered in wet bandages, could take innumerable types of mineral bath and generally ape their hypochondriac betters. But he was soon extending his propagandising to a wider audience and, in 1852, opened the Smedley Hydropathic. He and his wife were to publish a book explaining the various treatments and perhaps he will be most remembered for his spirited advocacy of the mustard bath. Smedley was not merely a hydropathic enthusiast, he was a positive zealot. Very soon his hydro was bursting at the seams and rivals began to open up other establishments nearby that all, to some extent, benefited from Smedley's reputation. On the religious side he was hardly as successful – building a large number of chapels which he gave to the Methodist Free Church and later revising the Prayer Book, but finding no church willing to use his version. He was also to patent a hydropathic baptismal font – but again found no takers.

Smedley did very well out of hydropathy and, in 1862, Ribber Castle was erected to house himself and his water-cure fortune. He could hardly have foreseen that, today, it would be used to house a zoo.

Matlock was not destined to survive as a spa beyond the 1920s. Smedley's Hydro is now the offices of the Derbyshire County Council and the other hydropathic establishments have all been put to different uses. But Matlock survives as a centre for Peak District touring; as an inland resort much after the fashion of Leamington, it stages attractions sufficient to bring in a large number of visitors which keep the many small hotels and guest-houses going. It also, along with a number of other places in Derbyshire, has its annual Well-Dressing ceremony which attracts a fair number of people itself and which still links the town to its distant origins as a watering-place.

The last of this net of Victorian spas to receive attention here is Lincolnshire's Woodhall Spa, whose advent dates from 1811 but most of whose development took place in the early years of the present century.

The mineral waters were discovered by accident during abortive boring operations for coal. The waters, containing iodine and bromine, are unique to Woodhall and, with the County Health Service still making use of them, Woodhall remains an active spa and a member of the Federation of British Spas. They are especially beneficial to sufferers from arthritis and rheumatism. Some early development took place here in the 1820s, but the resort did not achieve much beyond local fame until the 1890s. Two churches were built at either end of a shopping avenue, together with a number of large hotels and a Pump Room. In 1918 the large Victoria Hotel was destroyed by fire, many of its furnishings being removed to Petwood House which still functions as a hotel.

The town possesses a unique Kinema-in-the-Woods built in 1922 which, despite its secluded position, is only a few minutes walk from the Broadway. Woodhall Spa is no faded Regency gem, it is rather a small, twentieth century town in the suburban Surrey mould. Development has been slow and is mainly of the residential breed and it would be uninteresting on this score if it were not that Woodhall is relatively isolated so that its growth has a particular unusualness. It lies in wooded country between the fens and the wolds, its woods being a haven of birdlife and flora which elsewhere long ago withered before the onslaught of the pesticide pestilence.

5

Spa People

With few exceptions the majority of English spas were to owe a great deal to the efforts of various individuals who, in some cases, virtually created particular spas, and in others came to exert such a strong influence upon them that they came very much to mould both their life and reputation. In respect to the latter group the position of Master of Ceremonies – at least as interpreted by Richard Nash and his successors – was a ready-made spring-board from which a strong personality could inspire to and, in some cases, succeed in dominating the life of a spa town. Viewed from the opposite end of the spectrum, Dean Francis Close, who presided over the demise of Regency Cheltenham, could almost be described as a Master of Anti-Ceremonies.

Outside these confines the spas and their associated social life were to throw up personalities of their own such as George 'Beau' Brummel and, of course, the ultimate ornament of latter spa-life, the Prince Regent himself. The spas, however, considerably pre-dated the Regency. Despite the fact that his name came to be almost synonymous with the older centre of Bath, they also pre-dated Richard Nash. The spas really began to establish themselves in the last quarter of the seventeenth century. At this time, however, they were not really social centres but still places one travelled to to obtain a specific cure. Celia Fiennes I include here because she was a leading representative of this early age of the spa when taking the cure was not something done at a specific centre but as part of a nationwide journey.

Celia Fiennes was perhaps the greatest frequenter of English watering-places that the seventeenth century produced. She was a descendant of that Lord Saye and Sele who had been prominent in the councils of the more extreme

Puritan party during the Civil War and Commonwealth. But the Fiennes family had long been reconciled to the restored Stuart monarchy though, naturally enough, in the days of the 'Glorious Revolution' they were to back the Protestant Parliament and William of Orange. Celia was, herself, a severe anti-Papist. She was also a chronic hypochondriac and travelled the length and breadth of the country in search of water cures for her many complaints – a test of endurance which would seem to prove that they were hardly as debilitating as she liked to believe.

Celia made two extensive tours, one in 1686 and the other some eleven years later. Her comments are revealing, not only in relation to the various waters, but also in illustrating that England was still a very medieval society. Despite the cannons of the Civil War its towns were still largely walled, their streets narrow and ill-drained and in general being anything by hygienic. There was also, in her time, a marked disrespect for persons of rank, which she found very annoying. However, it was rather to be expected. The Civil War had put the English gentry at each other's throats and the spectacle of the leaders of local society pulling each other apart, both verbally and physically; had weakened the old regard which members of the 'lower orders' had previously held for them. It was not until the mid-eighteenth century that the strata of society really began to re-establish itself in English affairs, though that old reverence for position based purely on birth – which had been near religious in its application – was never to fully reassert itself. Celia Fiennes moved, to her discomfort, through a medieval landscape peopled by what may be termed fledgeling democrats.

Thus she has a lot to say about the behaviour of the local people at the various places she visited. At Bath the bath attendants were, from her point of view, pleasantly servile – but it was the servility of any body of people who relied upon the largesse of the wealthy for their livelihood. At St Winifred's Well, Flintshire she found the uncouth behaviour of the locals more difficult to swallow than the water and at Buxton did not like having to take the baths in the open with local farmers.

Far more to her liking were the watering-places of

Tunbridge, Astrop and Scarborough – though the latter seems to have been favoured as much because it had good lodgings run by Quakers than for any other reason. Tunbridge drew high praise because it catered for the gently-born with its coffee-houses, hazard rooms, bowling green and apothecaries' shops. Astrop had a similar air of elegance there being "a fine Gravell Walks that is between high cutt hedges where is a Roome for the Musicke and a Roome for the Company beside the Private Walkes". At Bath she was at pains to note that in the morning patients were brought to the baths in beize chairs and that, in the afternoon, their visiting was done in sedan chairs. To Celia such distinctions mattered much.

Her descriptions of the waters provide some insight into her own credulity as well as that of others. Harrogate's Old Sulphur Spring she noted as "a quick purger" with a smell that resembled that of a "carrion or a jakes". Nearby Copgrove Spa's St Mungo's Well "was exceedingly cold" and seems to have cured her of headaches before she resumed her travelling, which probably caused many more. Bath's water tasted like "the water that boiled eggs" while those of Buxton were "rather like milk". All over the country she came across adherents of the Old Faith busily converting wells into shrines. At Knaresborough she recorded that the local Catholics were ornamenting the well-side altar with flowers and digging for the bones of martyrs, while at St Winifred's the well had all the appearances of being a flourishing religious centre. From her lofty Puritan height she pitied them for not knowing any better.

Her record of her journeys at least proves that, by the end of the seventeenth century, there were many other nascent spas besides the two dominating, fashionable centres of Tunbridge and Bath. Some were destined to flourish in the following century and later, some to fade from even local popularity. But, at least, by the end of the seventeenth century England was already a nation of fervent water-curers.

Together with Bath and Tunbridge, Epsom was to be one of those early spas which was to survive into the eighteenth century. Its presiding genius at this time was to be the local apothecary John Livingston who emerges as one of the earliest men with ambitions to capitalise upon the attractions of a hitherto rather haphazardly organised spa centre. Not all that much is known of Livingston – there seems to exist no portrait of him nor a contemporary description – but he was obviously a man possessed of considerable business skill and ambition. Given the then popularity of Epsom as a spa, Livingston appears to have seen no reason why it could not develop to rival Bath. Buying up the old well, upon which the town's spa fortunes were based, Livingston was later to add shops, a bowling green and a pump room. Visitors of all kinds poured into the town and a new well had to be sunk to cater for their needs. But Livingston's interest was not confined to the spa's waters. In 1720 we find that "at Epsom is held a Market Weekly on Fryday, and 2 Fairs Yearly, Viz 24 July & 29th September, obtained & put in force lately by Mr John Livingston Apothicary in that town who is the present Proprietor of the Market and Fairs". Livingston had almost single-handedly turned Epsom from a village with a mineral water well to a thriving social centre.

After Livingston's death the spa continued to hold its own for some years and in 1773 a new well was opened, the Gentleman's Magazine stating that the taste of its waters was "rather nauseous and brackish, somewhat disagreeable, like to a stale egg". One can only wonder what attractions these exercised for Prinny and his entourage. However, mention of the future Regent takes us well ahead of Livingston's time and we must now return to the early eighteenth century and Livingston's contemporary at Bath, Richard Nash.

Richard Nash, perhaps the most enduring of all spa personalities and who was later to reign as the uncrowned King of Bath, arrived in the city in 1705 at the age of thirty-one. Already it was making its bid to oust Tunbridge Wells as the leading spa in the country and it was very much due to the influence of the 'Beau' that Bath succeeded not only in this aim but in far surpassing it to become for, at least a century, almost an alternative capital to London. When Nash arrived to become assistant to the then Master of Ceremonies, Captain Webster, he had already been through Oxford and had tried both the Army and the law – in the latter capacity having practised at the Middle Temple. Given his later life-style none of these earlier pursuits could have offered him satisfactory opportunities for the exercise of the ostentation he was soon to indulge so freely.

It was when Webster was killed in a duel at the gaming tables in the Town Hall that Nash first took over as Master of Ceremonies, a position he was destined to occupy for well over half a century. Webster's duties as Master of Ceremonies had been fairly simple, his responsibilities hardly extending beyond the gaming tables themselves. Nash, however, was soon to show that he considered the duties of the post extended into almost every quarter of Bath's social life – though, as he was to derive most of his income from a percentage cut of the banker's winnings, almost his first action was to set the gaming situation on a more respectable footing. It was Nash who now outlawed the wearing of swords at the tables – a safety measure he obviously considered a prerequisite for a Master of Ceremonies intent on a long run.

Just how the 'Beau' came to be acknowledged and accepted as the arbiter of Bath society must remain something of a mystery. It was, perhaps very largely a matter of personality – but, it was also because the upper strata of Bath society recognised that someone had to exercise what amounted to discipline at the spa. They would have found its exercise tedious and frivolous and were only too pleased that Nash had the ability to endow the traditional role of Court Jester with the dignities and ceremony that befitted the Augustan Age.

Nash also needed local support in his role and this was to be provided by such men as Dr William Oliver – whose coachman was later to net a small fortune out of his master's biscuit recipe. Oliver was concerned with the medical side of Bath's waters – and was closely associated with Nash in the foundation of a mineral water hospital for the local poor. Nash possessed something approaching genius in regard to organisation and political manoeuvre and it was he who, almost single-handedly, took on a rather laggardly corporation, persuading it to pave and clean up its streets and generally, in eighteenth-century terms, to put the city's house in order.

His *Rules of Conduct* were not drawn up until he was sixty-eight, and his grip on the expanding spa was by then beginning to slip. But he had already laid the basis of Bath's fashionable 'season' long before and, in some ways, the *Rules* were, by the time of their publication, already long-observed.

The Pump Room had been built in 1706 and Nash first began to extend his influence beyond the Town Hall gaming tables when he organised subscriptions for the maintenance and cleaning of the building. He was adept in mounting similar subscriptions for other amenities and when the first Assembly Rooms were opened in 1708 he organised subscription balls and concerts over which he, as organiser of these ventures, naturally presided. With the gaming tables already firmly under his control Nash now emerged as the fully fledged Master of Ceremonies, organising everything from the events at the theatre – founded by yet another Nash-promoted subscription list – to the music which accompanied the morning public-bath takers.

In Bath social regime as established by Nash was simple enough. Bathing took place at either the King's Bath or the Cross Bath before 10.00 a.m. where members of both sexes, suitably robed, soothed their bodies before taking breakfast either at the Assembly Rooms or at their own lodgings. This was followed by a visit to the Pump Room where three glasses of water were normally drunk – again to the accompaniment of music – and then most would attend morning service at the Abbey. Various pastimes, such as riding or driving in the Royal Crescent, then preceded dinner which would be taken around 2.30 to 3.00 p.m. Dinner would be followed by further visits to the Pump Room or to the Orange Grove with tea, around five o'clock normally being taken at the Assembly Rooms. In the evening there were a variety of entertainments ranging from balls in the Assembly Rooms – over which Nash generally presided – to concerts – where Nash had drawn up the bill – gaming – which Nash had organised – and the theatre – where Nash had engaged the artists.

It could be rather a boring round, repeated on this scale day after day. Everything, in fact, depended not so much upon Richard Nash, as upon the company in general. But, in the eighteenth century at least, this was never lacking and it was said that Bath provided for the needs of everyone from the most fastidious Methodist to the most licentious rake. Nash's major function, therefore, was not so much the provision of leisurely facilities as the creation of a social framework in which people of widely differing backgrounds and attitudes could nevertheless mix without treading on each other's social toes.

Nash was opposed to boorish behaviour, from all classes, on the ground that it produced dissention. His dictums were obeyed – even if they were resented – by visitors largely because they did result in making Bath a much more civil place. For many years Bath's social life was almost all conducted in public and the imposition of a general standard of behaviour was possible because it was essentially a very confined place. The adherence to Nash's disciplines prevented what could have been an unpleasant confrontation between the warring upper classes – the eternal conflicts between those who had power and money and those who merely had money.

Nash's fall from local grace came in 1739. For over thirty years he had reigned as the spa's titular monarch, quite often behaving almost as if he was one in fact. He was accustomed to appearing in the city streets in a carriage drawn by six greys, complete with footmen, outriders and announced by French horns. In his black wig, white beaver hat and floral patterned clothing made from the finest of materials he was not exactly unrecognisable to his subjects. He was now accepted completely, for it was generally believed that the elevation of Bath to the position of the most fashionable city in England was very much the work of the 'Beau', who seemed to have lavished his considerable attentions on the city as a labour of love.

The revelations of 1739 put an end to such delusions. Nash now discovered that some of his employees were taking more than their fair share from the profits of the gaming tables. Rashly he decided to take the matter to law. Most of Bath society was surprised and shocked. It seems that no one had ever really thought just how the 'Beau' managed to support himself in such style and when it was discovered that his

income came almost exclusively from gaming, Bath was outraged. He suffered a rapid fall from favour and was never quite to succeed in winning back his old ascendancy. Six years later Nash suffered a further blow when the Gaming Act of 1745 prohibited public gaming houses completely and forced the pastime behind the closed doors of private houses. But Nash must have derived some consolation at this time for it was in this year that he assumed the position of Master of Ceremonies at Tunbridge, managing to combine it with his duties at Bath as the two 'seasons' did not clash.

Richard Nash was ultimately to be succeeded at Bath by James Derrick who, by most accounts was not a greatly effective Master of Ceremonies. But the post was to live on for many years and was to be copied at most of the new spas, including early coastal resorts such as Margate and Brighton. Nash's influence, not only on Bath but on English social conventions generally, was incalculable. Even today the spirit of the man seems to survive in the gem of English Georgian towns.

Almost inseparably associated with Richard Nash in the fortunes of eighteenth century Bath were Ralph Allen and the father and son architectural team of John Wood the Elder and John Wood the Younger. Like Nash himself all could be said to have sprung from humble origins – and indeed the social climate of the spa towns was such as to make them, at this time, one of the most accessible areas for entry into the ranks of upper class society. It was Ralph Allen who was most responsible for putting the gilt on the 'Beau's' social gingerbread in the rising spa town. From its inception Prior Park, Allen's country in the town house, became the centre of fashionable Bath society outside Nash's round of public ceremonies.

Allen was a self-made man, a Cornishman who emerged into adulthood as a staunchly Protestant Hanoverian, convictions somewhat out of tune with the general feeling in early eighteenth-century, dissident, Jacobite Cornwall. In 1715 his position as a local post-master in the duchy brought before him important information that was linked to the Old Pretender's forthcoming Highland Rising. He relayed the information to General Wade, commander of the Hanoverian troops in the Highland campaign who, amongst other things, was also M.P. for Bath.

These were days when the concepts of 'interest' and service' were ingrained in almost all reaches of society – medieval concepts which still, to some extent, exercise their influence on modern British politics. Wade considered it only natural that he should reward Allen's service to the Hanoverian interest by a position within his own patronage. Thus Allen became postmaster for Bath, and was soon enjoying an influence on local affairs through a seat on the city corporation. Wade further rewarded the up-and-coming young man by bestowing upon him an illegitimate daughter in marriage. The general could hardly have done better as he was to remain a lifelong bachelor with only illegitimate offspring to bestow upon anyone. It was, however, quite within the social 'rules' of the time for members of the aristocracy to bestow products from the wrong side of the blanket upon promising young social climbers seemingly upon the consideration that half a leg up the ladder was better than none at all. In Allen's case, however, the arrangement was to amount to a considerable push, for, when Wade died, he left his martial fortune to Allen's bride.

In the 1720s Allen involved himself single-handed in a reform of the English postal system out of which he was to amass a personal fortune which he invested mainly in land and quarries around bath. At Combe Down he was to own the largest quarry for Bath stone and the remodelling and re-building of much of the city was soon to make it a vast show-room for his product.

John Wood the Elder, a Yorkshireman, was very largely responsible for the creation of Georgian Bath, much of his work being under the direct patronage of Ralph Allen. Although the elder Wood was to plan the grand design of the new city he died before its completion and much of the remaining scheme was to be undertaken by his son, John Wood the Younger. One of the elder Wood's greatest works in Bath stone was Prior Park itself, where work began in the summer of 1735. The house was constructed almost entirely of

Allen's trademark material – almost as if the great man was pointedly proving that anything that could be done in any other stone could also be done in that from his own quarries. With its dominant Corinthian portico it was completed at a cost of £240,000 – eighteenth century pounds it must be stressed – though its final embellishments were not the work of either Wood the Elder or his Son, but of Richard Jones, Allen's master mason. In later years Jones may have been responsible for the erection of Allen's Gothic 'folly', Sham Castle. Given Jones's early liking for the Gothic he seems more possibly to have been its creator.

Prior Park was soon to become the hub of fashionable Bath society and Allen was attributed with a character that bore some resemblance to that of the fabled Sir Roger de Coverley. In fact, Ralph Allen was to achieve some immortality in the pages of literature as the inspiration for Fielding's Squire Allworthy. He was renowned for his hospitality and patronage of the arts – something in which he was far from being alone amongst the wealthy of eighteenth-century England.

But, although Allen shared much with the great patrons of his time, such as the Littletons of Worcestershire's Hagley Hall and Lord Burlington, the great patron of Palladian architects, in many ways he was markedly dissimilar. Most importantly he was self-made and, to a considerable degree, self-educated too. He was modest, though not completely without ostentation, for Prior Park was as much a boast as a house. Allen, however, was a man of naturally good taste and this, coupled with his generosity and a naturally expensive intellect, made him a magnet for cultivated minds. This apart, Allen lived at Bath, the centre of the fashionable English world and, as its senior permanent resident, he acted as a natural nucleus for that centre. A list of those who were entertained at the house on the hill would only be tedious. Suffice it to say that, amongst political men of the day it was frequented by Pitt and Bolingbroke, whilst literary figures ranged from Alexander Pope to John Gay of *Beggar's-Opera* fame.

Those members of the traditional landed aristocracy who visited Allen's country seat above the town would not have been slow to appreciate that their host's rise to fortune and influence had been far different from their own. Older country seats had, in general, been the product of a fairly slow evolution. The manor house had, through a gradual process of addition, slowly evolved to the point where it had become the country house. In many cases, however, the eighteenth century had seen a violent end to the process. The country-house, the product of several centuries, had often been ruthlessly razed and the Palladian mansion had taken its place either on the same site or nearby. But, in almost all cases, one fact had remained unaltered. The country seat, whether house or mansion, had remained as the focal point of the landed estate, and had been the visible evidence of its owners wealth or position arising, in the first instance, as a result of his landed inheritance. Prior Park stood in no such surroundings.

Ralph Allen's home was built on a rocky eminence, surrounded by infertile soil which could not have maintained the livelihood of the most lowly of yeoman farmers. It was surrounded at first by no large estate though, in course of time, Allen did buy up much of the nearby land. Instead, it looked down a narrow valley toward Bath itself, from which Allen did indeed draw much of his wealth. After Allen's death Prior Park was to pass into a number of different hands and, before the middle of the nineteenth century, had become a Roman Catholic college. It still remains in the hands of the Church.

Together with Ralph Allen and Richard Nash, John Wood the Elder made up the triumvirate who first called fashionable Bath into existence. His architectural achievements – as well as his architectural dreams – remain to be discussed in another chapter. Yet it is very difficult to entirely disassociate them from his life and personality. Like Ralph Allen, with whom he was later to be so closely associated, he was very largely a self-educated man and was to be tremendously influenced by the revival of Greek and Roman styles as a basis of architectural design.

Wood practised as a surveyor in London and Bath before turning toward architecture. It was a move which was not uncommon in eighteenth-century England and the landscape gardener Lancelot Browne more than once deviated from his chosen path to stray into the preserves of the architect. Wood's side-step into architecture, however, was to place him there permanently and he emerged as one of the leading architects of the century.

Yet is was not so much Wood's actual realisations in Bath that are his greatest claim to fame. This must rest upon his overall concept of the creation of a Roman town on English soil. Given the tastes of the age and the popularity of Roman studies amongst the upper classes it was the perfect time for such a concept to be born. That Bath became the chosen site for this creation was natural, owing to the concentration of wealthy patrons in the city – most of them fully under the influence of the classical revival. Wood drew his architectural inspiration both from original classical sources and from their Renaissance developments. Coming to Bath in the late 1720s – probably at the initial invitation of Ralph Allen – he was inspired both by the city's own Roman associations and by the works of Andrea Palladio – the Venetian 'father' of the Palladian school of architecture – whose books were making an increasing impact on English architecture.

Palladio was the architectural hero of Lord Burlington – the leading patron of the new school of architecture in England. He had been one of the latest of Renaissance architects and one who had largely drawn his inspirations from the buildings of ancient Rome. Armed with an edition of some of Palladio's designs John Wood set about drawing up an ambitious plan to transform Bath into a latter-day imperial city complete with circus, forum and imperial gymnasia. It was a plan that hardly bore relation to costs and perhaps not all that much to the actual needs even of a very wealthy aristocracy. Much of the plan was never to be realised. But it was to form the basis of the Georgian city of Bath even after Wood's death in 1754. His grand plan was later to be largely adhered to by his son, who followed him in his practice, and by almost all subsequent architects in the city over the next three quarters of a century. It was very much due to the influence of the elder Wood that Bath was not to embrace the Gothic movement of later days with anything approaching the same enthusiasm with which it was received in most other parts of England.

Wood's most impressive achievement in Bath was the building of the first phase of his grand design which included Queen's Square, Gay Street and Brock Street. That he was not an architect of overall excellence is proved by his work on the Mineral Water Hospital which was promoted by Dr Oliver and lavishly financed by Frederick, Prince of Wales. Wood was a visionary – and if the realisation of his vision was a practical impossibility, then he came as near as any man to having the fabric of his dreams transcribed into reality. The Bath that has long been the admiration of the world was once largely the figment of one man's imagination. The city was indeed blessed in that there existed in the years of its renewal a man of such imagination as John Wood.

Compared to the exertions of Nash, Allen and Wood, the efforts of many other erstwhile spa promotors seem puny indeed. Yet it must not be forgotten that Bath was a spa long before the eighteenth century and, no matter how splendidly they built, the three men did not have to face the formidible task of laying an original foundation. This apart, once Bath did achieve the position of being England's off-duty capital, it was to serve as the model for many later spa towns. Imitations almost always compare badly to the real thing, at least until they arrive at the point where they begin to develop some individuality of their own by which time, of course, they can afford to be judged on their own merits.

Henry Skillicorne had some acquaintance with Bath, and more with the Clifton Hot Wells, before he retired to Cheltenham with his wife and family in 1738. He was later to be described as a "tall, erect, robust and Active" man, "never once intoxicated" and, by the time he met Elizabeth Mason, who was to be his second wife, he had already lived the most adventurous of lives. In fact, his pre-spa activities read like a scenario for *Treasure Island*. He was by origin a Manxman and had, naturally enought for anyone brought up on the island, made his life the sea. He had become captain of a merchantman trading chiefly into the North American and Mediterranean ports – where he had had more than one skirmish with the Barbary Corsairs – and had built up a considerable personal fortune. Later he retired to Bristol where, at the age of forty-nine, he was to meet and marry Elizabeth Mason. Elizabeth's father, William Mason, had retired to Bristol from Cheltenham some years earlier. At Cheltenham he owned land on Bayshill, including that on which stood the Old Spring which he had had enclosed and canopied some years before, though it had later become derelict and neglected. When William Mason died Elizabeth and her captain moved to Cheltenham with their children to take up the Mason inheritance.

Skillicorne was not slow to recognise the potential of the Old Spring. In his opinion Cheltenham could easily become a successful spa town if only it could be sufficiently beautified and publicised. In conjunction with a scion of the Berkeley family, Narborne Berkeley, Lord Botetort, he laid out Well Walk leading from the town to the approach to the well-head Pump Room he now built. For some decades Skillicorne's Wall Walk was to remain one of the major features of the spa, a long avenue lined with elms and limes and giving a fashionable rural vista across the neighbouring countryside. The Walk passed close to Grove House – popularly known as 'Mrs Field's' and where there was gaming and dancing. For many years this was to share with the Pump Room the position of 'leading social resort'. 'Mrs Field's' was also a commodious lodging house, which tended to syphon-off the cream of the early spa's visitors.

The captain's dreams of expansion and possible competition to Bath were given fresh impetus following the publication of Dr Short's *History of Mineral Waters* in 1740. Short claimed that the Cheltenham waters were the most effective in the country and, largely on the strength of this, the captain now predicted a rapid rise for the new spa. It is certainly true that Cheltenham owed its initial rise as a spa town to the efforts of Henry Skillicorne – but little remains to show for his efforts today. What is seen by the modern visitor to the town is very much the creation of later years. Undoubtedly Henry Skillicorne had the energy to give the spa its beginnings, but he was hampered by two major factors in going much beyond the stage of initial inspiration. One of these was the insularity of the local population, who resented the change he was attempting to foist upon them. The other was undoubtedly the fact that he was already well beyond the prime of life when he first undertook his Cheltenham designs. Henry Skillicorne was forty-nine when he first came to Cheltenham and, though he lived to the age of 84, his active life in promoting the new spa extended for little more than a decade. Given the difficulties he had to face he just did not have the time to convert his dreams into realities.

By the time that he died, in 1763, it would have seemed that Cheltenham was never destined to become a spa at all. The captain had apparently long before given up all hopes of his schemes ever reaching fruition and it was to be left to his sons, the Rev Richard Skillicorne, William Skillicorne and various other enterprising promotors to take up his ideas and convert Cheltenham into the Midland playground of the Regency. Somewhat less than two decades later Cheltenham had advanced to the position where it had not one but two masters of ceremonies. In the person of William Miller, a Londoner imported by William Skillicorne to superintend functions at the Long Room adjacent to the Old Well, Cheltenham had had its master of ceremonies for some time prior to 1780. In that year, however, Simon Moreau appeared on the scene and the town appears to have immediately split into two rival camps of elegance.

The next three years were to witness a battle for supremacy between the two men which Moreau was destined ultimately to win, not so much because he was the better candidate but, it would seem, because he, unlike Miller, did not have a directly commercial connection with any of the infant spa's facilities. Moreau and his wife faced the severe hostility of Miller and Skillicorne and if, at first, it had appeared that he would not be able to establish himself in the town in the event he was to preside over it for the thirty years prior to his death in 1810.

At the time of Simon Moreau's arrival in Cheltenham the town was still very far from being a serious rival to Bath. Whereas Bath's visitors were now more than two thousand annually Cheltenham could still claim to draw them only in their lower hundreds. But Cheltenham's season was to grow steadily in importance until it came to be the rival not of Bath, which it came to eclipse, but to the social capital of the Regency, Brighton itself, Simon Moreau was not an innovator. As former Master of Ceremonies at Bath he had been greatly influenced by his predecessor Nash – and was only one example of how much the Beau's Bath regime was aped by the later spas. The 'Rules of Conduct' he imported to Cheltenham were so closely based upon those pronounced by Nash as to be virtually interchangeable.

By later standards Moreau would have been adjudged a fop. Yet both the foppishness of Moreau and Nash was a necessity for the time. Someone had to set the tone for places which, in the earlier years of their existence as spa, were patronised by a wide cross-section of society. On this score Simon Moreau acquitted himself very well. In later years the spas tended to become more exclusive places with a tradition of elegance which the masters of ceremonies had done so much to establish. But, once the tradition had been created and 'polite society' had become an established fact, it was almost a natural development that spa society would become increasingly fastidious, finally to the point where it was able to dispense very largely with the services of the masters of ceremonies themselves. Increasingly spa society began to move out of places of public ceremony and into their own private social circles. The reign of the masters of ceremonies was over – but the standards of social behaviour which they had once proclaimed almost as if they had been the edicts of kings remained to permeate English society for well over a century. In so many ways they are with us still.

This consideration of Simon Moreau and of the influence of masters of ceremonies in general has been put rather ahead of the advent of the presiding genius of early Malvern, Dr John Wall. Wall was neither a flamboyant leader of society in the mould of Richard Nash nor an ambitious spa promoter in the likeness of Henry Skillicorne. Rather he was an eighteenth-century man of science, whose work at the Royal Worcester Tonquin Manufactory was to bring him in touch with some of the leading scientific and philosophical thinkers of his day including Mathew Boulton, James Watt, Priestly and other members of the Lunar Society. It was an age when the cultivated man aimed to encompass all the leading forms of human expression, and when science and art were not necessarily viewed as being in opposition – the worst excesses of the Industrial Revolution which would place a gaping abyss between art and applied science, were yet to come.

John Wall's interest in Malvern was basically medical tinted with a faint touch of commercial exploitation. He knew the area intimately and had been born at the Severnside village of Powick on the Malvern side of the river in 1708. The medicinal wells of Malvern had retained a local reputation dating from the Middle Ages and young John must have grown accustomed to ailing locals deciding to tramp across Malvern Chase to drink of the healing waters of St Anne's Well and Holy Well. When he came down from Oxford to set up in medical practice in Worcester it cannot have been long before his mind turned to the wells and their reputed powers as a cheap means of curing the illnesses of some of his poorer patients. The real impetus was to come when he became a founder member of the Royal Worcester Infirmary which catered largely for the poorer people of the town. If the wells were really as good as their reputation declared then there could be no objection to local people taking 'the cure' and probably getting as much good out of it as those who could afford to patronise the growing ape of Captain Skillicorne's nearby Cheltenham.

Wall, however, was true to the scientific outlook of the age. In cooperation with William Davies, a local apothecary, he decided to give the water of the various wells a serious analysis before recommending their general use. Samples of water were taken from St Anne's Well, the Holy Well and the chalybeate spring and subjected to trials in Wall's laboratory attached to the Worcester Tonquin Manufactory – a concern which was later to earn greater fame as the Royal Worcester Porcelain Company. His results were to be published over a period of fourteen years, culminating in the publication, in 1757, of *Experiments and Observations on the Malvern Water*. This included an analysis of the water of the various wells together with details of some of the many cures which had been attributed to their waters. Analysis had shown that the wells contained very little mineral content, but that they were also remarkably free from impurities of any kind. Wall attributed their beneficial effects almost solely to this latter fact declaring that "the efficacy of this water seems chiefly to arise from its great purity". As a somewhat natural consequence of Wall's discovery one local writer was to say that,

The Malvern water, says Doctor John Wall,
Is famed for containing just nothing at all.

However, given that most urban drinking water in eighteenth-century England was likely at almost any time to give rise to outbreaks of typhoid and kindred epidemics, Wall's declaration was certainly not an inimportant one. But, at the same time, his publications were not unattached to a desire to popularise the Malvern waters and at the same time to improve the amenities already existing for visitors. He was the prime mover in establishing a committee of local Worcester gentry to raise subscriptions for the improvement of accommodation at Malvern, and this was later to result in the extension of Well House which had been built in 1761. He was active in seeing that the walks were improved and also in making the wells accessible to his patients from the Royal Infirmary. In 1773 new baths were provided, again by a subscription fund launched by Wall.

From all this it can be seen that John Wall, far from emulating the fashionable regime of Nash's Bath, was an ideal precursor of Drs Gully and Wilson. His activities at Malvern were almost exclusively devoted to its medical aspect, even to the point where he originated the bottling of local waters for patients too ill to travel to the wells themselves. It was largely to be left to others later to graft the first real social fabric upon what, in Wall's time, was still very much a small village at the foot of the Malvern Hills.

John Wall retired from Malvern in 1774 at the age of sixty-six. Appropriately enough he left to go to Bath. He left behind him an infant spa that was still to be in business when most of the spa facilities of the older centre had long sunk into decay. His mark was felt on local society in other directions, notably in the Tonquin Manufactory – where he had discovered a process for making porcelain. Under his direction the company was to see its most prosperous and inventive years, producing work which was justly claimed to rival that of the Continent. In his *History of Worcestershire* a copious, two-volume work finished toward the end of the eighteenth century – the local historian, Dr Treadaway Nash (no relative of the 'Beau') eulogised the many talents of the Jacobite Doctor. He died in Bath in 1774 and was buried in the abbey where his commemorative plaque still stands.

Perhaps because of its concentration on the medical, rather than the social aspect of spa-life Malvern was destined to flower as a Victorian hydropathic centre rather than as a Regency spa on the lines of Cheltenham or Leamington. Both towns threw up Regency characters of their own. Yet it would be true to say that the centre of Regency social life was not to be found in the Midland spas but at the spa-by-the-sea of Brighton. Life here was naturally dominated by the Regent himself, holding court in the newly completed Royal Pavilion. Yet, if the Prince Regent was the titular head of Regency life, there was another whose influence on social affairs was, for a relatively short period, almost as great.

George Brummel, like most of the spa people so far considered, came from humble stock. His father had been a clerk in government service who later became private secretary to Lord North at the time that North was Prime Minister and presiding over the break-up of the first British Colonial Empire in the American War of Independence. It is probable, however, that his grandfather had been a personal servant – perhaps a valet. George's father, however, did well enough to send his son to Eton. It was the springboard of the college that was to give George a relatively easy passage into the Assembly Room of Regency aristocratic life.

At the time the tradition of sending boys to boarding school had not yet become the established upper class practice it was to be by the latter decades of the nineteenth century. Many aristocratic families still clung to the older tradition of the private tutor and the Grand Tour as the basis of their childrens' education. But the tradition of the boarding school was growing. No less a personage than the Duke of Wellington was to imply that Eton was the perfect training ground for the future army officer – and it was the military life to which George Brummel was initially drawn. But Wellington's famous remark about Eton's "playing fields" did not refer so much to sportsmanship as to the pitched battles between rival groups of pupils that, at this time, seemed to be a feature of the College. Reform was urgently needed at many of the older schools – something which the rising middle class were pointedly to imply in the foundation of their new system of proprietory education. Yet reformers were not yet on the scene – the most well known, Thomas Arnold of Rugby, was not to begin his headmastership until the second decade of the nineteenth century.

Leaving Eton George Brummel was to secure a commission in the Prince of Wales' own regiment, the Tenth Light Dragoons. Shortly afterward he was to make what, in the jargon of the day, was regarded as a 'good match' – though it was not a wealthy one. It would seem that Brummel met the Prince long before he entered the regiment and long before the Prince became Regent. He was already carving out a reputation for himself as a wit who had brought the studied social insult to the status of a minor and accepted art. His manner was affable and his personal appearance – which embodied what may be described as a cool and well-tempered arrogance – was somewhat more apparently aristocratic than the factual aristocrats were able to create. He was, therefore, a near-perfect ornament for Regency society. Brummel was the antithesis of the Regency fop. If Richard Nash had been alive in his day the two men would soon have crossed swords for Brummel thoroughly disapproved of the florid style of both dress and manners which Nash had promulgated at Bath and elsewhere. Brummel's social style was the ice-cold elegance of disdain. It was a style which held its dangers, not only for those who might fall foul of the Brighton Beau's acid tongue, but also for Brummel himself. Brummel was bound to make enemies but ultimately it would appear that there was only one man he could not afford to have as an enemy. This was the Regent himself who admired a witty tongue as long as it was not directed too sharply toward him. It was a situation that Brummel ignored at his peril. But ignore it he did and there began to appear a widening rift between the Prince and the Beau which, combined with his one intemperate activity, gambling, was to ultimately lead to his fall from grace.

In the summer of 1813 Brummel and three of his friends, William, Second Baron Alvanley, Henry Pierrepoint and Sir Henry Mildmay, won a considerable amount at the gaming tables. They decided to throw a ball to mark the occasion at London's Argyle Assembly Rooms and, though Brummel and the Regent were no longer on speaking terms, it was considered that the Prince ought to be invited. The Prince duly came but, when the four hosts were standing to receive their guests, he pointedly ignored Brummel and Mildmay – with whom he was also on bad terms.– but shook hands with the two others. As the Prince was about to enter the ballroom Brummel, resenting the snub, called out 'Alvanley, who is your fat friend?' The Prince never took references to his proportions – which by now were considerable – very kindly and this remark, coming from Brummel, was enough to sever the last threads of their relationship. The two former friends were never to speak to each other again, although they were to meet twice more, in accidental circumstances from which the 'Beau' each time managed to extricate himself with his old coolness.

But Brummel was, by now, heavily in debt and the friendship of the Prince could have meant much to him. But he was not by nature inclined to grovel for favour and decided, as did many impecunious Regency figures, to quit England for the safety of France. He settled at Calais later moving to Caen and living in deepening poverty. He began to neglect his appearance and, cut off from his friends, began to fall into a steadily worsening state of mental depression. His last hope of a reconciliation came when the former Prince – now King as George IV – visited Calais in 1821 *en route* to Hanover. Humbled by poverty Brummel may have thought that the new dignity of kingship may have led his old friend to a display of magnanimity. Through his valet Brummel presented the king with a bottle of a liqueur which he knew he had been partial to in the old days – it was all he could now afford. But the king was to ignore Brummel's gesture and perhaps could not bring himself to renew the acquaintance of a man who had so insulted him. The King moved on to Hanover and Brummel was left to shift for himself as well as he could. But the 'Beau' was a broken man. He died in a French asylum in 1840.

By 1821 the former Regent was far from being the carefree leading of society he had been a decade earlier. The spirit of Regency life was indeed to live through his reign as king and through that of his brother, who reigned as William IV. But the Prince gave no more to the social life of England. His greatest bequest had already been made in the creation of the Regency coastal spa of Brighton.

As we have already seen the rise of Brighton as the popular resort of the wealthy and influential was to deal a death blow to the wider social life of, most obviously, Bath, Tunbridge and Cheltenham. The northern spas of Buxton and Harrogate were rather beyond its pale of influence and tended to continue their growth, while later spas, such as Malvern or Llandrindrod were not in competition as they tended to concentrate their efforts more on the medicinal side of affairs. But the more southerly spas found that their leisure-and-pleasure facilities could not cope with the new seaside fashion, especially when Weymouth, Margate and a host of other places along the south coast began to exploit their seawater attractions. Even the northern spas were to come under some threat from the rise of Cromer, Redcar and Bridlington and the conversion of Scarborough from spa to coastal resort.

The Prince of Wales was a man of mixed tastes and mixed abilities. The whole of his adult life was to some extent to be spent in a spirit of reaction to his upbringing and especially to his father. George III may not have been the most politically adept of monarchs, but he was a zealous family man. He was also respected for his apparent simplicity and lack of affectation and was, toward the end of his active reign, to gain considerable affection from his subjects in general who were to dub him, not unkindly, 'Farmer George'. But his domestic affairs were conducted with some despotism, with great frugality and considerable repression. If the Prince of Wales emerged into manhood not exactly hating his father it was certainly with a determination to live a life far different than that which his father had been able to impose.

But, no matter how ostentatious he was, no matter how wild or frivolous his activities, the Regent, explicitly in his position, lived out his nine years as caretaker-monarch with his father's shadow at his elbow. He did not become king until 1820 and the fête of Regency England was always haunted by the spectre of the mad king. Many people could never forgive him for living a life which appeared a studied insult to his sick father. For them, perhaps the Prince should have spent that nine years in semi-mourning. But, given his character, that is something which would have been completely impossible. In many ways the Regent wanted to disassociate himself from George III as much as possible. From this viewpoint London remained largely as the old king's capital – depopulated of the Court for long periods and without royal power – while Brighton was to become the social and political capital of the Prince's regency. The Pavilion was its nerve-centre and it was here that the great figures of the day were expected to wait attendance on Prinny.

But all was not politics – far from it. The Prince was as good a watercure fanatic as the next man. He had drunk it at Bath, Tunbridge and other places and had drunk and bathed in it here. When the Pavilion was built he instructed that sea-water be piped into the royal baths. Lesser mortals had to take their chance with the original element, bathing from the bathing machines which were hauled into the water as far as safety would permit.

But, after 1820, his last ten years appear as a rather sad decline. Although he admired wit he was not a wit himself and slowly most of his early friends were to forsake him. He was to suffer greatly from gout – a general affliction of this heavy-drinking age – and from increasing bouts of illness of all kinds. His once slim figure had, even by 1813, become more than merely rotund – as George Brummel had pointed out.

But, by 1820, it had swollen to alarming proportions so that in this respect at least he came to resemble the bloated Henry VIII. Trips to London were made so that he arrived in darkness and he was carried in a litter so that people would not be able to tell if he was still capable of walking on his own two feet.

Illegitimate children he had fathered with considerable generosity – but he produced no heir to the throne. It saddened him to realise that he would not be succeeded by a son but by his brother William whose years on the throne (1830-1837) were to form, in retrospect, the Later Regency. The Prince suffered by never really being the father of his time, being always, to some extent, no more than a substitute for a king. He was perhaps the Regency's greatest ornament. While he did not leave his stamp on it, it left its stamp on him.

As the Regency and the Regency spas died – partly as a result of a social levelling process which brought the rising middle classes to both the older spas and the newer coastal resorts, a new form of spa, the hydropathic centre, arose to take over many of the medical functions of the spa. These spas of the Victorian years were in general dominated by a new breed of man, for the commercial spirit of the entrepreneur had by now spilled over from the trading and manufacturing base of the Industrial Revolution to embrace most forms of English life. The catchword of 'progress' had replaced the traditional concept of patronage. The newer spas were not aristocratic. They were middle class. The aspirations of those most closely concerned with them were middle class also.

Typical of this breed of 'new men' was John Smedley who, in the mid nineteenth century, almost single-handedly put Matlock into the front rank of spa towns. At the age of thirty-seven John Smedley was a textile tycoon of wide and extravagant tastes. His fortune had been made at his hosiery works at Lea Mills, Derbyshire and, in 1840, he considered that it had sufficiently made him a gentleman of means to merit his taking the leading aristocratic diversion of the day, the Grand Tour. Accordingly he set off for the Continent but, whilst in Switzerland, he contracted a fever accompanied by all the signs of a mental breakdown. Smedley may have been a tycoon, a captain of industry possessed of phenomenal energy – but he was essentially an exhausted man. During the previous fifteen years he had nursed an ailing family business back to vigorous life to the point where it was now one of the leading enterprises in its field. It had meant ceaseless work and the effort had taken its natural toll. Smedley was advised to rest and to travel – contradictory advice which produced no good at all. Finally he returned to England and was persuaded to enter the hydropathic establishment of Ben Rhydding in Wharfedale near Otley. From here he was to emerge not only physically reconstituted but spiritually reconstituted also. Besides having been converted to hydropathy as a means of dispelling all physical ills he seems to have been simultaneously converted to Methodism as a means of dispelling spiritual imperfections. Armed with these two weapons of ultimate truth he set out to practise his beliefs upon his unsuspecting workforce at Lea Mills.

At Lea Mills Smedley launched a campaign combining cold water treatments with spiritual texts upon his reluctant workers. The cold water douche system was augmented with wet-sheeting, wet bandages and dew-walking. To some extent this was to be offset by the Smedley educational system which involved the building of two schools and half a dozen chapels of the Methodist persuasion. As few of John Smedley's workers can be claimed to have been ill at the time he introduced what could be called the people's cure, it is rather difficult to estimate what good, if any, it actually did them. But certainly, daily immersion in an atmosphere liberally impregnated with religious fervour, would have had some effect. That the effects were noticeable may be judged from the fact that Smedley was soon being encouraged to provide facilities for the treatment of those who would normally have striven manfully to disassociate themselves from anything that had originally sprung from a connection with the lower orders. Smedley's middle class patients were soon outnumbering those unwilling recruits from the Lea Mills manufactory and the fervent hydropathist was to open premises especially to cater for this new inflow – Smedley's Hydro – at Matlock Bath in 1852.

Smedley's conversion had led him to believe in the frugal life and, reputedly, to despise luxury. But having once, at the onset of his religious conversion, disposed of his wordly goods, he was, as a result of his hydropathic endeavours, soon to acquire others in even greater abundance than before. By 1862 hydropathy had provided John Smedley with a fortune even greater than that he had derived from his textile interests. In this year he saw the completion of the mock-Gothic pile of Ribber Castle which, perched on its rocky height, overlooked the town of Matlock and in which he was to live in not inconsiderable elegance.

At his Matlock hydro, Smedley toned down much of the original 'cold water treatment,' as it had been practised at Lea Mills – the middle-class being considered to be of a more delicate disposition than the Lea Mills workers whose rigorous working lives were obviously thought to fit adequately them for almost any torment. More than two thousand patients, on average, attended the Matlock Bath hydro annually and dutifully paid attention to Smedley's strictures regarding the wearing of clinging, abrasive merino wool suits by children – and adults if sufficiently submissive – and the regular taking of mustard baths. Mustard baths were something of a Smedley speciality.

John Smedley's wife, Caroline, was a willing partner in her spouse's schemes. At the time of John's conversion to water and religion she had undergone an equally rigorous conversion in apparent sympathy. She aided John in the running of the Matlock establishment and went somewhat further by supplementing his enterprise with the compilation of a home hydropathic manual for women. This did not neglect to mention the most suitable hydropathic measures to be observed on the honeymoon. The Smedleys were nothing if not thorough.

Smedley's Hydro was well-patronised by the clergy – who were to be the mainstay of many a hydropathic establishment in later years. At his death John Smedley's practice was to pass to his protegé, Dr William Bell Hunter and the town, which had now sprouted a number of similar establishments, continued to prosper as a spa centre for some decades. But there is little left at Matlock to remind one of John Smedley today. Ribber Castle is now a zoo and Smedley's Hydro houses the offices of Derbyshire County Council. Smedley and his water revolution are now definitely pieces of the historical and moribund past.

There was a passing resemblance between some aspects of the career of John Smedley and his contemporary John Corbett who laid the foundations for Droitwich's fortunes as a spa. But, while Smedley seems to have merely transferred his natural industriousness from textile manufacture to hydropathy in both enterprises being in overall command, Corbett's relationship to the spa functions of the town with which he was most closely associated was largely that of the philanthropist. In this he was more in the pattern of Bath's Ralph Allen than Matlock's John Smedley.

Corbett, even more than Smedley, was almost the typical Benthamite entrepreneur, the mid-nineteenth century captain of industry with philanthropical leanings. By dint of personal energy and enthusiasm he revolutionised both the traditional industry and fabric of a town where both had remained substantially unaltered for centuries. He was, in the case of Droitwich, almost a one-man industrial revolution, succeeding in evacuating from the town an industry which had been established there since before the Roman occupation.

Corbett had already tried the engineering industry and canal freighting before he turned his attentions to salt manufacture. At the time that he began the initial borings for brine at Stoke Prior, a few miles to the north of Droitwich, he knew very little about the industry in the development of which he was to play so large a part. But John Corbett was a fast learner. Some of the early bores proved abortive, but he sold his interest in his canal boats and persevered. Ultimately he was to be rewarded by bores which tapped a river of brine of both greater quantity and greater purity than that being extracted at Droitwich.

Stoke Works began to take shape and very soon had become the new centre of the local industry. This was very far from being the age of the modern-day commuter and Corbett set about building a model village for his employees incorporating, besides the houses for the salt workers, a dispensary, rest-rooms, reading-rooms, a school for employees' children and a library, all revolutionary provisions for their time. Naturally a large number of workers moved from Droitwich to the new site and, with the salt industry being slowly concentrated there, those that remained were to find it increasingly difficult to obtain work. With his salt processing plant now firmly established Corbett began to turn his mind to the possibility of providing Droitwich with an alternative means of existence. A local outbreak of cholera had been instrumental in proving the medicinal qualities of the local brine and Corbett bent his interests to promoting this as the basis for the town's future.

He created a new Droitwich to live alongside the old industrial centre. This was a Droitwich that pursued life as a serious health resort, many of its new hotels being complete with suites of baths and its life centred upon the St Andrew's Baths built at Corbett's direction. Besides spending much of his money in giving Droitwich a new function and a new future he was also to provide the capital for, amongst other things, Bromsgrove Cottage Hospital and for extensions to the new University of Birmingham. One of the town's architectural wonders is Chateau Impney, which stands a little out of the town to the right of the road leading toward Birmingham. The chateau, copied from the design of one of those in the Loire Valley, was built by John Corbett for his French-born wife. Corbett was to later sell out his interests in the local salt trade to the monopolistic Salt Union – and probably lived to regret his decision. In an attempt to push up the price of salt the Union cut-back production in the Droitwich area, producing unemployment on an unparalleled scale. But John Corbett was now an old man and had left the chateau to retire to Wales.

Here he was to make a determined effort to turn the North Welsh coastal village of Towyn into a Victorian resort. He was responsible for the creation of the sea-front promenade where commemorative plaques still record that not only did he provide the esplanade but its sun-shelters as well. In fact the town with its Corbett Arms Hotel, Corbett Vaults, Corbett Avenue and the rash of plaques recording his generosity is, in some ways, a better memorial to the man than the Droitwich he changed so radically. However, despite his spacious promenade and the Assembly Rooms – now the local cinema – Towyn was not destined to become a booming seaside resort. The sea-front promenade was roughly half-a-mile from the old village and, until relatively recent years, attracted little building to fill up the gap. Modern housing is now beginning to knit the area together, though Towyn's present-day popularity would seem to depend not so much upon its nearness to the sea, but on that to the two narrow-gauge railways, the Talyllyn and the Fairbourne. But, before he left for Wales, John Corbett had firmly laid the basis of Droitwich's development for the next fifty years. Without his interest it would probably have been left to languish as one more decayed manufacturing town.

If John Corbett's interest in spa-town Droitwich was that of the philanthropist and that of John Smedley in Matlock was that of a particularly frenetic spa promoter then the concern of last of the spa people to be mentioned here had much more basic inspiration. George Dawson of Harrogate was a speculator. Beginning his career as a builder George Dawson was to net a personal fortune out of Harrogate's rise to become the leading of English late Victorian and Edwardian spas. His childhood and youth are irrelevant here, for Dawson has been included to give some small insight into the in-fighting and shady-dealing that often went on behind the elegant façades of the spa towns right up to their post-1918 fall from grace.

Most of the earlier spas had been built almost entirely by private enterprise and Harrogate differed from these in its latter phase by mixing both private and municipal enterprise, with the latter coming increasingly to dominate. George Dawson was the foremost amongst a group of local builders who were to do very well out of Harrogate's spa expansion in the late Victorian years. Behind the scenes he managed to cope with Harrogate's chaotic political system and to secure himself some very valuable contracts. There was considerable protest over the way various projects were awarded in the town, but George Dawson was never to be directly implicated in any scandal.

But he was certainly a man with an eye to the main chance and perhaps the rather tortuous history of the Montpellier estate best serves as an illustration of his capabilities. In 1867 Fredrick and Joseph Thackwray — sons of one of the main creators of the post-Regency spa — formed the Harrogate Hotels, Mineral Springs and Bath Company Ltd., to operate the nucleus of the old spa's attractions, the Montpellier Baths, Pump Room and Gardens as well as the Crown and White Hart Hotels. When this company failed after only a couple of years of life it passed to its mortgagee Tom Collins M.P. for nearby Knaresborough. Collins now sold it to Dawson who extended the hotel facilities and added a skating-rink to the Montpellier complex. By 1880, however, the enterprise was obviously heading for trouble and Dawson formed the Crown Wells House Hotel Company to cover it with himself as chairman. Within two years this company had gone broke — largely as a result of lavish overspending on providing creature comforts for residents. Somehow Dawson seems to have evaded any responsibility for the company's failure and even turned up as one of the liquidators. Two years later he bought the Montpellier estate for £19,750 well aware that there were distinct possibilities of it being bought and developed as a municipal enterprise in the near future.

Harrogate was now on the brink of becoming a Borough and Dawson swung his considerable weight in favour of the town's incorporation, which was granted in 1885. Within three years the new Borough had decided to enlarge and improve its existing spa facilities and bought the Montpellier estate from Dawson for £29,500. His four years ownership of the estate had thus netted him a profit of just short of £10,000. Alderman George Dawson was later to be duly acclaimed as one of Harrogate's 'Worthies'. He was a man of power and influence and a symbol of the self-interest which lay just below the surface of the grand designs of many a spa town.

The two centuries between the journeys of Celia Fiennes and the activities of George Dawson cover a social period which could be described as the age of the English spa. It would have been impossible to include here all the diverse characters that the spas threw up. I can only hope that those included, some of necessity only briefly, in some respects illuminate not only themselves but the times in which they lived.

6

The Coastal Spas

The evolution of the English coastal spa was a slow and very gradual process. Its real beginnings may be assigned to the mid-eighteenth century, though it must not be imagined that no one had ever bathed in sea-water before this. They had – but it was not until this time that the practice had been raised from the depths of the vulgar to something which was compatible with 'fashion'. Once George III had entered the waves off Weymouth in 1789 the new passion for sea-bathing was never to look back.

As distinct from the sea-side resort proper – which was to be a development of later, largely Victorian times – the coastal spa was confined almost solely to the south coast. Following Weymouth came Brighton – which was to reign supreme during the Regency – with Margate, Ramsgate and Worthing not far behind. These merit the description of coastal spas partly on the grounds that here sea-bathing took the place of bathing in public or private baths, partly because they drew their initial social inspiration from the inland spas with assembly rooms, circulating libraries, coffee houses and so on and partly because they adhered, in their early years, to that peculiar spa institution, the Master of Ceremonies.

There were exceptions to this south coast domination, such as Cromer and Blackpool. But the most obvious exception was Scarborough which had long functioned as a spa beside the sea – though with the presence of the waves as the least of its original attractions.

Scarborough had been in the spa-business since the beginning of the seventeenth century. Its mineral spring had been discovered on the foreshore – where its waters had discoloured some nearby rocks – by a Mrs Farrow whose

fervent publicity regarding their application had soon made it
a haven for the ill-disposed amongst the Yorkshire gentry.
However, popularity in those distant times, was not to be
reckoned in thousands and for some decades Scarborough was
to enjoy only a modest flow of annual visitors. It was not until
the beginning of the eighteenth century that the spa obtained
its first set of purpose-built buildings and it was during these
years that it really began to succeed as a spa.

Sea-bathing seems to have begun here as a fashionable
pastime earlier than anywhere else. Reports from the 1720s
mention mixed bathing parties using the beach, normally
from the shelter of tents or awnings – a precaution not so
much against the curious but rather against the keen wind.
Rather more daring spirits took to the sea in small boats and
plunged into the sea from these, the men usually naked but
the women wearing a loose fitting 'water-robe' which was
gathered at the neck. By the third decade of the century
progress in the cause of decency had proceeded as far as the
creation of two changing rooms on the beach, one for either
sex.

Some of Scarborough's grander architecture, such as The
Crescent, seems to owe something of its inspiration to Bath. It
is certainly true that Scarborough was attempting to become
the northern Bath and, for many years, faced little
competition, for infant Harrogate was then still the poor
relation of neighbouring Knaresborough. Yet the inland resort
was to up-stage it by the end of the century and Tobias
Smollett, of *Humphrey Clinker* fame, was to detect a falling-off of
its popularity in favour of Harrogate by the end of the 1770s.

"The Queen of the Northern Watering Places", as it was
advertised, was not to regain some of its old pre-eminence
until the coming of the railway. The age of the day-tripper and
the fortnight by the sea had arrived. But it was never
Scarborough's intention to become merely another sea-side
resort. After all, it was a spa with all the fastidiousness that
the term now implied. It aimed to cater for the better-off sea-
side visitor and, in the late Victorian period, this aim was
backed up by local builders who were to build such imposing
edifices as the Grand Hotel for the holidaying Victorian

middle-class. Nonetheless, it was always to be rather outdone by its rival and, in many quarters, was never to succeed in losing its popular appellation of "Harrogate by the sea".

The south coast sea-side spas were something quite different. They were entirely new creations, none having previously had a spa function. In relation to Bath, the nearest inland resort of note, Tunbridge Wells, had been ailing for some years and thus, when first Weymouth and later, and more effectively, Brighton appeared on the scene, there was no inland resort near at hand that could be claimed to offer effective competition. This apart, Weymouth arrived, like most eighteenth-century spas, largely as a result of royal patronage. Brighton received royal patronage in a massive dose, not only from the presence of the Prince of Wales, but from the earlier residence of his uncle, Ernest, Duke of Cumberland, and subsequently from almost all of his relatives. Such a fate was never to be visited upon relatively genteel Scarborough.

Royalty was to desert Weymouth almost as soon as it arrived. A local speculator, fearing for the royal constitution immersed in the local waves, built a sumptuous bath near the shore at a cost of £500. But George III was to use it only once, though that is not to say that it was wasted money for it was to be heavily used by those who flocked to the new-found resort in succeeding years. There have been few who have considered that the king's liking for sea-bathing was indicative of his approaching madness.

Weymouth's continuing royal patronage was to be closely linked to the king's bouts of temporary insanity and it might be said that when he finally became permanently deranged, Weymouth largely dropped out of the royal picture. The king took to convalescing at the resort after his earlier visitations and continued to visit it as long as he was able. Just how closely fashion followed 'Farmer George' may be judged from the sudden fame and popularity of nearby Christchurch Bay where the king took to the water as a change from Weymouth. Modern Bournemouth owes its origins largely to this distant royal visit – though the intrusion and sudden notoriety of the spot was doubtless hardly welcomed by the local smuggling fraternity, including one Isaac Gulliver who led a particularly successful band. These sported white livery and called themselves 'The King's Smugglers' – claiming the authority of the king for their activities given, it was said, in return for Gulliver's assistance in supplying information about Jacobin plots against the monarchy. When Isaac Gulliver left the 'trade' he retired to Poole where, appropriately enough, he ran a local wine shop. It would hardly have been surprising if it was well-stocked with contraband liquor.

Brighton's rise to fame dated from the late eighteenth century when the Duke of Cumberland took a house on the Steine – the broad sweep of clifftop grassland that looked out across the English Channel. It was still a modest fishing-village and still generally referred to as Brighthelmstow and was not to begin to develop into the Brighton of today until the Prince of Wales decided first to buy and later to have a house built there. The famous Pavilion grew rather than was built.

But the Brighton bonanza must not be all attributed to the presence and influence of the Regent – though this was reason enough, given the eighteenth-century and Regency notion that fashion was largely something set by the Court. It was generally aided by the publication, in 1752, of *A Dissertation on the Use of Sea Water* by a local Brighton doctor, Richard Russell. Russell declared that certain disorders benefited not only by sea-bathing but by sea-drinking – a notion that found a reasonable acceptance amongst people already accustomed to downing their daily three pints of saline water at the inland resorts. Some few years later another Brighton doctor, John Awsiter, was to declare that sea-bathing was good for numerous diseases and might even cure infertility. He took what was generally accepted to be a scientific approach to the new treatment, declaring that its rigours were too great to be undergone by children or those past middle-age, that it was unwise to bathe after a heavy meal and that the best time of day for entering the water was at dawn when both mind and body were in a calm state. John Awsiter established the first off-shore baths at the new resort.

The writings of these doctors, and of others, helped not only in the growth of Brighton, but in that of other resorts as well.

But Brighton was to profit most, largely because it was already gaining itself a fashionable reputation.

It must be said that sea-bathing in the late eighteenth and early nineteenth centuries was far different from the modern pastime. It was, primarily regarded as a medicinal exercise and only very secondarily as a recreational one. Strictly speaking, sea-bathers were not expected to enjoy the sea, though, no doubt, many did. Many people did not really bathe at all. Instead they 'dipped' – hence the origin of the term 'to take a dip'. They were lowered into the waves by local Dippers, of whom Brighton's Old Smoaker was perhaps the most famous. It was Old Smoaker who gave the infant Prince of Wales his first dip on the Brighton foreshore. Others used bathing-machines – which were hauled into the sea either by men or horses. But many bathers were not so fastidious and there are numerous reports of mixed naked bathing parties at Brighton, Scarborough and other coastal spas in the late eighteenth century. Naturally, as time wore on, Queen Victoria and her prudish subjects were not amused by the practice, which gradually died out – though, as late as the 1870s, we find the Rev. Francis Kilvert, of 'Diary' fame, wearing only his birthday suit to brave the waves off Shanklin.

Brighton's rise to the status of a royal spa town began in 1779 when the Duke of Cumberland took a house on the Steine. The Duke had long ago fallen out with his brother George III, largely on the grounds that the King had objected to his marriage to Lady Anne Luttrell who had Irish Catholic connections. This, to the King, seemed to pose a threat to the Protestant throne and, to counteract it, he promoted measures which barred any member of the royal family marrying under the age of twenty-five without the consent of the monarch. These measures were to present the Prince of Wales with particular difficulties in relation to Mrs FitzHerbert.

The Duke, naturally enough in the circumstances, allied himself with the King's Parliamentary opponents, the Whigs, and took the side of the Prince of Wales in his struggle against the domination of his father. Partly as a result of the Duke's influence the Prince was also to align himself with the Whigs. The Duke was a sporting, relatively intelligent member of the

Hanoverian family who heartily detested the stuffiness of his brother's court. The Prince also resented his father's influence and, when the time came, Brighton seemed the obvious place to which to flee.

The Prince, however, could not do so without his father's consent, until he was twenty-one. As the king considered the Duke of Cumberland the most disreputable company such permission was hardly likely to be forthcoming and the Prince did not make his first visit to the Duke's Brighton home until he was indeed twenty-one, in 1783. It was to mark the beginning of an era.

The town was growing steadily, though it was still basically a fishing village whose fishermen caused some annoyance to fashionable visitors by stringing their nets across the Steine so that the ladies especially found it almost impossible to walk there. The situation was later remedied when the Steine was enclosed, a fence being erected along it and the local fishermen thus losing their ancient rights. They protested – but to no avail.

By the time of the Prince's first visit the town was already well on the way to becoming an established resort. There were fashionable houses, dominated by those of Dr Richard Russell and the Duke of Marlborough. The latter's was originally built by Samuel Shergold, the proprietor of The Castle Inn, for letting to fashionable visitors but was bought by the Duke in 1771.

Social life revolved around the Assembly Rooms of the two major inns, the Castle and the Old Ship. In the daytime their places were taken by the circulating libraries, of which by this time, there were three, the oldest being that of a Mr Baker, formerly of Tunbridge, which had been established as early as 1760. These libraries were far more than their title suggests, for they were gossiping rooms, billiard rooms, bazaars and reading rooms as well – the ideal place to meet friends and arrange parties for later in the day. Besides the balls at the Assembly Rooms there was a Sunday Promenade and Public Tea and numerous card-playing assemblies.

Fashionable Brighton had imported its own Master of Ceremonies to oversee these activities. Captain Wade was said to have succeeded James Derrick as Master of Ceremonies at Bath and for a few years to have presided over Bath's winter season as well as Brighton's summer one. But, from 1770, he was based entirely at Brighton and exercised much the same sway over Brighton society as Beau Nash had once done at Bath. Nash, however, had never had to compete with the Prince Regent and, once the Prince began to make ever-more frequent visits to Brighton, the Captain's importance began to wane. In 1808 he died to be succeeded by William Forth, who was considered to be an irrelevant upstart by the proprietor of the Old Ship Inn who refused to have the new Master of Ceremonies on his premises. But the office did continue to have its uses, the Master of Ceremonies serving for many years to unite the visiting society, arranging introductions and generally smoothing the path for new arrivals. The office was not finally abolished until the 1840s.

By the time the Prince of Wales paid Brighton his first visit the resort had already attracted such prominent personalities as Defoe, Gibbon and Johnson. In the wake of the Prince more literary figures were soon to be added including Burke and Sheridan and later, the young Lord Byron.

By 1800 Brighton's resident population had risen to more than 7000, a figure which was considerably inflated by the visitors of the summer season. There was considerable building expansion to provide houses for those wishing to stay in the town – but of these early buildings and of those of the true Regency period (1811-1820) few remain. In fact the only surviving actual Regency building of note in Brighton today is the Pavilion itself – most of the other Regency buildings being largely erected in the immediate post-Regency period (1820-1836).

Socially Brighton was to boom following the establishment of the Brighton Camp. This was a military encampment on the open land behind the town, first created in the spring of 1793 in readiness to repel the expected French invasion at the outbreak of the Napoleonic Wars. The invasion, as we know, never came – but the summer camp became something of an annual fixture, attracting unmarried women from all over the South searching for handsome husbands in military scarlet.

The Prince of Wales, as Colonel in Chief of the Prince's of Wales' Own Regiment, took a prominent part in the military displays and parades – and, once, even did a spell as officer of the watch. It was from this time that he began to rather fancy himself as a martial Prince. In later years – while not exactly contradicting the fact that the Duke of Wellington had taken some part in the downfall of Napoleon at Waterloo – he came round to the opinion that the Allied victory had been largely won as a result of his own advice and efforts.

If Brighton could not, by its very situation, claim to be a spa in the truest sense of the word, it did its best to make up for the disadvantage. Sea bathing and sea-water drinking had taken on a spa-like function since the earliest days of the resort's existence, but in the early 1880's, attempts were made to provide the town with bathing establishments that might be the rival of any inland spa. There was some need for these as many visitors had expressed offence at being confronted with the spectacle of naked bathers on the public beaches and, in general, the new indoor establishments were to observe the proprieties with some rigour. Brighton's first indoor bathing centre was that established by Dr Awsiter in 1769 and which survived as Creakes' Baths until its eventual demolition in 1861. A rival made its appearance with William's Royal Hot and Cold Baths on the Steine and, in 1813, a third establishment appeared as the Artillery Baths which, after various extensions over the years, was eventually to be incorporated into the Grand Hotel.

The town's most renowned indoor baths, however, were Brill's, standing at the foot of East Street. Originally known as Lamprell's they had acquired their new name when a nephew of the founder took over their running. Charles Brill, the new owner, also established a bathing centre for women on the site of the old Awsiter Baths and it was here that Queen Mary, the consort of George V, is said to have first learned to swim. Brill's Baths outlasted the First World War and were not pulled down until 1929 when they made way for a cinema.

But the establishment which most vied with the later treatments to be offered at the surviving inland spas was run by an Indian of the unlikely name of Sake Deen Mohamed.

Sake Deen had seen service with the East India Company and, with them, had received some training in surgery. Later he took ship and arrived at Cork where he was to run away with a young Irish girl, arriving with her at Brighton in 1786. His establishment was a complete departure from the hot and cold water baths offered elsewhere and, at first, was largely ignored by the resort's fashionable visitors. His treatment rested on the vapour bath and subsequent massage – the latter then being more commonly known as shampooing. Following the bath, massage was applied in complete privacy to the patient who lay shrouded in a flannel tent into the sides of which were let two long sleeves of material to admit the shampooer's arms. Sake Deen was not one to take the public's disregard lying down. He was a considerable publicist and began to air the 'cures' he had performed, the result being an enormous pick up in trade. In later years he was patronised by the Regent and was appointed Shampooing Surgeon to George IV in charge of the bathing suite at the Pavilion.

In many ways Sake Deen's treatment was an early precursor of the way many of the inland spas were to go later in the century. In the mid-1860s a Turkish *hamman* much influenced by Sake Deen's earlier success, was set up in Brighton and very soon similar *hammans* – or Turkish baths – were springing up all over the country.

One reason for the pre-eminence of Brighton as a coastal spa was, not so much the presence of the Regent and the reputed powers of its sea-water, but the efficiency of its transport system. Visitors multiplied in almost direct proportion to improvements in communications between London and the coastal towns throughout the late eighteenth and early nineteenth centuries. Following the opening of the Brighton Road – at one time there had been a number of variously tortuous routes – and with the arrival of the new Royal Mail coaches, Brighton became almost a fashionable suburb of London. The road developed a mystique all its own and became famous for its races between aristocratic young bloods who often took the ribbons of some of the more famous coaches.

No other coaching road could rival the fame of the Brighton

Road – not even the Great North or the Dover Road – but its hey-day was not much more than a decade. In 1841 the railway arrived at Brighton to link it with London by a journey that took a mere two and a quarter hours. Despite valiant efforts by some coach-owners to stay in business traffic was to desert the road almost overnight and – apart from the occasional race – it was not fully to revive until the coming of petrol-powered transport.

The coming of the railway coincided with Brighton's decline as a coastal spa and the thoroughgoing extension of its more legitimate development as a seaside resort. Day trippers now began their summer invasions of the town. They were not exactly a new experience for the South Coast – trippers of one sort or another already formed a large proportion of visitors to Southend, and Margate had long been served from London by the Margate hoys – sailing ships loosely modelled on the Thames sailing barges. With the coming of the railway it was no longer possible to maintain the regular stratification of society that had been such a feature of the more recent years of both the inland and the coastal spas. The beach, promenade and Brighton's Chain Pier were now the main attractions of a 'day by the sea' and not the circulating libraries, assembly rooms and off-shore baths.

The impossibility of regulating the social life of the many varied visitors was admitted at Brighton when it abolished the post of Master of Ceremonies. All around Britain's coasts resorts were springing up, only a few, such as Blackpool and Cromer, having had any claim to have developed from spa beginnings. The coastal spas merged with the newer seaside resorts which grew up at the rail termini and, by the mid-1850s had, apart from fringe developments, passed out of the mainstream of spa development altogether.

7

Spa Architecture

At the outset I think I should say that in this chapter I am confining myself to discussion of that architecture which was occasioned almost solely by the spa functions of the towns included in this volume. Thus I shall not include the multitude of religious buildings – not even Bath Abbey, for it was hardly originally built to cater for the needs of spa-goers – nor the schools, but will stick to those buildings which would hardly have been created if the towns had not first and foremost, been spas.

Spa building covered a period of roughly two centuries, ranging through Queen Anne to Palladian, Regency, Victorian Gothic and, in the case of Harrogate at least, to municipal Gothic. Of Classical and Regency styles the spas of those periods contain some of the most perfect examples to be found anywhere in Britain.

In the earlier fashionable spas the existence of certain buildings designed for specific functions was something of a prerequisite to them being called spas at all. Assembly Rooms, gaming rooms, coffee houses and the circulating libraries were to become almost the aggregate edifices upon which most spas rested. But the literal fount of their activities were the Pump Rooms – and there were few spas which did not possess at least one; at one time Cheltenham had no less than three.

Of course, pump-rooms were not always deemed a necessity. Tunbridge Wells did very well without one for many years and at Bath water-drinking, as against bathing, did not develop to the point where it was to acquire fashionable premises until the beginning of the eighteenth century. Later, in the nineteenth century, hydropathic resorts, such as Malvern and Droitwich, offered their waters largely in private as against public places and, though Tenbury Wells was to prove a marginal exception to the general rule, many latter-day spas, such as Church Stretton, did not go further than providing ornate drinking-fountains or, at best, covered well-heads as at Shap Spa.

Tenbury Wells' cast-iron Pump Room, erected in 1862 and designed by James Cranston – whose best work is also to be found in Worcestershire at the Teme Valley village of Shelsley Beauchamp where he was responsible for the major re-building of the church of All Saints – deserves to be dismissed here before considering the splendid structures of earlier years. The Pump Room stands off the main street, Teme Street, behind the Crow Hotel. It is designed something after a Chinese pagoda – but do not expect to find anything along the lines of that in Kew Gardens. Cranston was long past his prime and the Tenbury Pump Room is a mean affair and cannot have looked very well even when it was new. Today its baths and showers are closed as a danger to the public and the whole structure is rapidly rusting away – on windy days bits of Oriental iron-work scrape and rattle to give it even more of a forsaken air. It seems something of an insult to places such as Bath and Cheltenham to have their magnificent edifices sharing the same descriptive function as this weird, ill-conceived and cheap-jack building.

If spa pump-rooms can be said to have English lineage then this must be traced to that at Bath. The present building was designed by Thomas Baldwin, Bath City Architect, and erected in 1790 to replace the earlier pump-room on the same site and which had been opened the year before Beau Nash's arrival in the city. Thomas Baldwin had already made an impressive addition to the Old Pump Room in 1786 when he had designed the Ionic loggia to screen the Abbey Churchyard from Stall Street and this was retained to be incorporated in the new building.

Of course, there were pump-rooms in existence before 1790 – but few worthy of the name have survived and none in their original form. That at Tunbridge has been demolished while the pump-rooms at Leamington, Buxton and Cheltenham all date from the early nineteenth century – Cheltenham's Pittville not putting in its appearance until 1830. Of the earlier failed-spas only the Georgian Pump Room at Melksham deserves a mention while, of latter-day entrants to the league, there is that of Ripon erected in the early years of the present century and doomed to near-neglect because of the proximity of booming Harrogate and to rapid oblivion in the wake of the First World War.

Bath's Pump Room shares with the city's Guildhall the distinction of being one of the two finest buildings that Thomas Baldwin was to erect in the city. The Guildhall was opened in 1775 to replace the earlier, decayed seventeenth century building and marked the opening for Bath of what, now that the Woods were no longer in business – John Wood the Younger died this same year – may be called 'the Baldwin era'. Baldwin had been working with Bath builders for some time, but nothing of especial significance emerged until he was entrusted with the Guildhall. His reign, however, compared to that of the Woods, was not to be an unrivalled one. Men of lesser abilities had never been able to challenge the supremacy of the Woods but Baldwin, good architect though he was, was to be surrounded by a number of others whose abilities were the equal of his own. The Woods were Bath's architectural monarchs – Thomas Baldwin was the leader of an architectural oligarchy.

The Pump Room was built in the Classical manner, its interior, with its great Corinthian three-quarter columns, being a triumph of Grecian achievement. The Classical style was superbly maintained at the Pump Room's front on to the Abbey Churchyard and Baldwin went further by improving the area with the rebuilding of the wall of the Cross Bath and by the creation of the colonnaded Bath Street – the only street in England to be colonnaded on both sides.

The Pump Room is now one of the major attractions of tourist Bath. It is an elegantly proportioned building with its elliptically arched recesses at each end and its lofty, coved ceiling. The green and gold colour-scheme maintains a subtle air of elegance.

Chronologically, of those pump-rooms which have survived

to the present day, the next major one to appear was Cheltenham's Montpellier. This arrived in 1817 but it was not until 1826 that Cheltenham's leading Regency architect, John Buonarotti Papworth was commissioned to add the famous domed Rotunda. A branch of Lloyd's Bank now carries on its business in the building. The Rotunda is supported by sixteen Corinthian pilasters and, at the time of its building, was described as 'a circular room, fifty one feet in height, and fifty in diameter.'.

Regency Pump-rooms were also erected at Buxton, and Leamington – but that at Buxton was later demolished to be replaced by the present Pump Room built in 1894. Leamington's Pump Room dated, in origin, from 1808 and was only saved from demolition in the 1860s by a spirited galvanisation of local interest in which the local newspaper, The Courier, played no small part.

Cheltenham was to be the scene of the erection of the next spa-pump room that has been left to us. This was the Pittville Pump Room – or Pavilion – opened as the centre-piece of the newly-created spa-suburb of Pittville in 1830. This magnificent building, designed by the local architect John Forbes – though some authorities maintain that Papworth also had some hand in its construction – was destined to become something of a mausoleum for the fast disappearing glories of the spa. Even now the local council may consider that it is something of a white elephant.

The new pump-room was designed as the centre-piece for a new spa creation which would be entirely divorced from and in direct competition to Cheltenham, which already had its own pump-rooms in the form of the Montpellier and the now-demolished Sherborne Spa.

The Pittville Pump Room stands on an elevation backed by the Cotswold Hills and approached from the High Street through terraced streets and a network of formal gardens. It has the proportions – and originally the appearance – of a temple rather than the traditional pump-room. Forbes designed this Classical monument with a frontage of Ionic columns, the building being of two storeys surmounted by a dome – it is the dome which has seemed to suggest the involvement of Papworth. Within the lower floor functioned as either a hall or ballroom with the spa, in which was housed the drinking fountain, opening onto its northern side. A circular gallery provided a promenade from which spectators could watch the dancing and also opened up to the domed roof, giving the pavilion a feeling that was nothing short of palatial. In July 1830 – almost as if to celebrate the downfall of France's restored Bourbon monarchy – the new pump-room was opened at a public breakfast presided over by Captain Marshall, the then Master of Ceremonies. Joseph Pitt, the spa's promotor, must have looked forward to great things for the Pittville. But they were not to come. Cheltenham was in slow decline and the Pump Room was destined to be used mostly for the occasional concert and ball. Pittville never succeeded as a spa and, in Cheltenham as a whole, drinking the waters was no longer the thing.

Matlock, Droitwich and Malvern were, in a non-alcoholic sense, bathing as against drinking spas. Here hydropathic treatments of one sort or another formed the basic elements of the 'cure' and water-drinking – at least in public – did not develop far beyond the prescribed glasses at an essentially outdoor well-house. At Malvern, for example, the sophistication of the Georgian and Regency pump-room regimes would have been completely misplaced. Malvern was no ally of the traditional water-cure, but of its up-and-coming rival – the Gothic brand. Not for Malvern gentle music in elegant, neo-Grecian halls, but an imported German band oompahing with all its Bavarian might while the infirm, but stoically enduring clients – originally provided with alpenstocks – took their Graffenburg glasses at the open St Anne's Well halfway up the hillside. Given this atmosphere it is hardly surprising that Pump Rooms were omitted from the hydropathic spas.

Buxton, however, was rather differently placed. Here was a bathing and drinking spa that only latterly developed into a hydropathic centre. Together with its thermal baths Buxton's St Anne's Well had formed the basis of the spa since its earliest days. It had been William Cavendish, Fifth Duke of Devonshire, who laid the basis of the present spa and who employed the Yorkshire architect, John Carr, to build the Crescent and the Stables, the latter now incorporated within the Devonshire Royal Hospital. The original St Anne's Well was almost within the arms of Carr's Crescent. In 1854, a double pump-room was erected which stood for forty years before it, in turn, was replaced by the present Pump Room, given to the town by the Seventh Duke of Devonshire.

The Pump Room now functions, more prosaically, as the town's Information Centre. Designed by Henry Currey, who was also the architect of the Palace Hotel, it stands in The Crescent and its exterior cannot be said to be particularly interesting. The north side was at one time arcaded, but this was later enclosed in a subsequent reconstruction. At the time of its construction the new Pump Room was in infringement of the original Enclosure Act which had declared that access to St Anne's Well – which the Pump Room claimed to contain – must be free. As visitors to the Pump Room were required to pay for the privilege the Act had obviously been disregarded and, to honour the letter of it, a free pump was later placed a little to the west of the building. Just over thirty years ago this was replaced by the present pump. Spa drinking water is no longer freely available – nor hydropathic cures, which can now only be obtained privately at the Devonshire Royal Hospital. But this is not to say that Buxton's waters are still not taken, though admittedly only by accident. The town's new swimming pool uses the famous blue mineral water and there must be many a local swimmer who has gulped down the 'cure' involuntarily. At least, it must be presumed, it keeps the local children from becoming early arthritics.

If Harrogate was later to be known as a centre for the hydropathic cure it was not to lack its Pump Room. This arrived in 1835 as a backward glance to the Classical style of the Regency spas and in 1842 Isaac Strutt, a local architect, designed a rival in the domed, octagonal Royal Pump Room.

Harrogate prospered as a water-drinking spa almost as much as a bathing and hydropathic one. In August 1898 31,546 glasses of water were served at the Royal Pump Room and 52,851 was the total number of glasses taken during the month at the leading pump rooms combined. In 1901, during a single August morning, 1800 visitors took the waters at the Royal Pump Room between 7.00 a.m. and 9.00 a.m. Pressure on the Royal Pump Room became so great that in 1913 the original building was extended by an annex.

The Royal Pump Room still exists – now functioning as a museum – but the original Pump Room, or to give it its full title, the Royal Promenade and Cheltenham Pump Room – was to disappear shortly before the Second World War. This had been one of the few spa buildings at the resort which had any claims to architectural distinction. But Harrogate was now in the depths of depression, the spa trade seriously on the wane and the pump room – maintained, like most of the other spa buildings, by the local municipal authority –·was felt to be an unjustifiable drain on the local rate. It had been the largest of Harrogate's public rooms containing, beside the pump-room itself, a large saloon and a library. Its frontage incorporated an elegant Doric portico and the building stood imposingly in six acres of garden. Its loss must be seen as a disaster, for it was a building which provided Harrogate with a readily recognisable link to the great days of the earlier English spas.

On architectural merit alone Harrogate's western rival, Bath, has claims to rank as the greatest of all the spas. But I have my doubts as to whether this is really a just assertation. The eighteenth century flowering of Bath could only have occurred because the city had been first and foremost a spa. Yet, in comparison to other spa centres, it was far more than just another watering-place. Bath was already a provincial capital in days when most other spas-to-be were still little more than villages – and certainly in the days when Tunbridge was something verging on a courtly version of the modern-day Caravan Club. The fact that most of the leaders of late seventeenth-and eighteenth-century English society journeyed to Bath had the effect of making it virtually a second metropolis.

The creation of Classical Bath was, therefore, far more than merely the creation of a spa town. The vision of John Wood the Elder was no less than the total recreation of a Roman city on English soil and it was hardly more than a series of historical accidents that led to Bath becoming the chosen site. But it was the already existing fashion for taking the waters that was most obviously to lead to Bath's later architectural development. Fashionable society, and political and artistic society as well, flocked to do worship at the latter-day shrines to Sul Minerva. There was already a Roman tradition about the place – though just where no one was quite certain as the Roman remains were to stay largely undiscovered until the middle years of the nineteenth century. If there had to be an ideal place in England to create a city on Roman lines then Bath was it.

Many of Bath's Classical buildings were to have no direct association with the spa as such. Along with Wood the Elder both Thomas Greenaway and John Strahan of Bristol designed a large number of buildings, most of which were created as private residences or lodging houses, though in 1707, it was Greenaway who was responsible for the erection of the new Cold Bath. Wood the Elder was to complete only a very small proportion of his plan for the city, most of which was later to be undertaken by his son with, to some extent, augmentation by other architects who tended to follow the general principles behind the original conception.

It was to be John Wood the Younger who largely created the Classical city between 1754 and his death in 1775. Within the wide scale of his activities in the city his major achievements were three in number. The first two – the Circus, completed in 1765 and the Royal Crescent, completed in 1775 – were obviously not what could be termed essentially spa buildings, but are so much part of the life and soul of Classical Bath that it would be a sin to omit them here. The third, the new Assembly Rooms, completed in 1771, became the very hub of the Bath society over which the successors of Beau Nash were to preside.

In origin the Circus was the conception of the Elder Wood, who died before he was able to execute it. It was an integral part of his Imperial plan for the new city, its inspiration most clearly derived from Rome's Colosseum. While the original Colosseum is an oval the Circus is a perfect circle with each of the three segments having their three orders superimposed with Corinthian at the top, Ionic at the centre and Roman Doric at the bottom. The Corinthian storey had the Elder Wood's garlands and cherubs heads while the parapet is crowned with sculptured acorns. On the architrave of the Doric order is something which may be a distinctive contribution to the Circus of Wood the Younger. Here there are hundreds of small, sculptured metopes, not once repeating themselves and all beautifully created. Flowers, masks, weapons and a host of other things – including unwanted pigeons – fill over three hundred places. It must be said, however, that the elements and atmospheric pollution have, between them, certainly helped to detract from the original beauty of the Circus.

While Wood the Younger may have been following his father's plan for the Circus rather closely – even slavishly – it is not so likely that the same was true for the Royal Crescent, his next monumental work in the city. The Crescent was indeed an important part of Wood the Elder's original plan, but it is unlikely that he had worked out its precise specifications before his death. At all events work was not to be begun upon it until thirteen years after his death. By this time John Wood the Younger had matured as an architect in his own right and it would have been well nigh impossible for him to have undertaken the work – even if there had existed a detailed design – without firmly imposing his own imprint upon it.

The composition of The Royal Crescent, seems to mark the Younger Wood's emergence as an architect in his own right. Its composition is of an order which far surpasses anything that the Elder Wood attempted – at least on the grand scale – and, as if to emphasise that another architect was here making his real debut, its inspiration is not to be sought in Imperial Rome but in the Renaissance Rome of the Vatican. In the general design the architect appears to be drawing his inspiration from the colonnaded piazza of St Peter's, though Wood uses the Ionic order while Bernini's great work had been in Doric. Wood would certainly not have had to travel to Rome to see Bernini's work – it and many others were readily available for study in the pattern-books which dictated the course of so much English Classical architecture.

The Royal Crescent was deliberately designed with as little ornamentation as possible. Indeed, of English Classical buildings on the epic scale, it is the one which most relies upon the perfection of its sweeping lines to achieve its effect. The Crescent has no centre, unless the two close-spaced columns surrounding a single round-headed window can be said to justify the term. But this is by no means cited as in any way a defect. Wood obviously wanted nothing to mar the sweep of the Crescent, and if a defined centre-piece is missing then so is pedimentation of any form, even the doorways being plain and the whole composition free of architectural clutter.

The Royal Crescent suffered marginally in the air-raids of the Second World War and some of the houses of the Circus were burnt out by incendiary bombs. But this was nothing compared to the fate that was to overtake the New Assembly Rooms, which were gutted by fire in a particularly ferocious raid in 1942. Happily the city fathers decided not to let this become one more unbecomingly redeveloped site – for which Bath Corporation otherwise seems to have a peculiar enthusiasm – and after the war steps were taken to ensure the building's eventual restoration. It was re-opened in 1962 with its interior as faithfully reproduced as modern materials and craftsmanship would permit.

The two main rooms of the Assembly Rooms were the ballroom and the great card-room. In the days immediately before the disastrous bombing the card-room was known as the Tea Room and this name has been resurrected for present-day use. Wood's two-storey range of columns at the western end – Ionic supporting the Corinthian columns of the gallery – luckily survived the fire and the fine ceiling has been reproduced under the direction of Oliver Messel who was responsible for the re-created interior of the whole building. Corinthian columns also figure in the ballroom, where Wood was at pains to omit any unnecessary decoration siting recesses for statues, urns and musicians well up the walls so that they did not encumber the general sweep of the room. At Bath even the tone of the Assembly Room's music may have been said to have been fashionably elevated. Although the ballroom is very much a reproduction job the essential spirit of Wood's design has been carefully recaptured and, at least, the five chandeliers are genuine period pieces being made by William Parker of London in the year of the Assembly Rooms original opening.

Beau Nash died ten years before the new Assembly Rooms were opened. These were, instead destined to be the Courts of Bath's latter-day monarchy, James Derrick and James King. Nash had presided over Bath society at the assembly rooms generally known as the Lower Rooms – or Wiltshire's – built by Wood the Elder in 1728 and later rebuilt by William Wilkins in 1810. Here there had been a portico in fifth-century Doric following, not the accepted Grecian lines, but those of buildings in Hellenised Sicily. (Wilkins had a personal passion for the style – the Magna Grecian.) Unfortunately the building was gutted by fire – by accident as it was a little too early for German bombers – and was later to become the site of the Literary and Scientific Institution, which managed to incorporate the surviving portico into the new building. It was, however, only a temporary survival for the Literary and Scientific Institution bit the dust between the two world wars and its Magna Grecian portico was carted away on a series of developers' lorries.

Although the two Woods are generally described as 'of Bath' their buildings were in a far less provincial mould than those of others who were to be predominantly associated with the locality as was Thomas White at Worcester. In fact, their building was of a national rather than a provincial stamp and would not have been out of place in the metropolis, for Bath was now truly London-in-the-West. Yet, it must be said, that it was very much because Bath had been largely a provincial city with a medieval inheritance of cramped building crammed into a relatively confined space that the work of the Wood's rose with all the effects of grandeur. Apart from the Abbey itself the early city possessed nothing on the lines of the monumental. If their work had been undertaken in London, while it would have been far from lost, it could have never hoped to transform it as it did Bath. Even in the mid-eighteenth century London was already too large to permit of a metamorphosis even by architects as talented as the Woods. Bath, on the other hand, was small. It was the nation's second capital. It had a Roman past. These, and other considerations perfectly fitted it to have a Roman present.

Apart, perhaps, from Tunbridge in the late seventeenth and early eighteenth century and Brighton in the early nineteenth century, other spas did not primarily come to exist as social capitals on the lines of Bath. They were dominantly leisure, pleasure and health resorts and the architecture they produced was confined to reflecting these preoccupations.

Leamington's rising popularity produced, in 1812, the Regent's Hotel – then regarded as the finest building of its kind in Europe – and the Prince himself came over for its opening from Warwick Castle. Other building proliferated on the northern side of the Avon and, in 1812, appeared 'The Parthenon' with a fine Corinthian portico. The building was later to be re-christened the Assembly Rooms.

In the South East Princess Anne, later Queen, had provided the money for Tunbridge's Pantiles as early as 1700. But, with a few exceptions, major spa buildings were not to appear at the resort until the early years of the nineteenth century. Thus, while Tunbridge is amongst the first of English spas, it shares with the rising spas of the early nineteenth century a considerable legacy of Regency architecture.

Tunbridge's great fortune was to attract the services of the rising young architect, Decimus Burton, who had already designed a number of terraces at Regent's Park as well as designing the Ionic screen at Hyde Park Corner. It was not, however, the original intention of those who employed Burton and his brother James to do anything to enhance the attractions of Tunbridge. Their intention, like that of Joseph Pitt at Cheltenham, was to create a new town that would first rival and then the eclipse the older one. However, Calverley was to share the same fate as Pittville and was destined never to sever its umbilical cord with the older centre.

To this period belong the Claverley Hotel – once known as Claverley House and frequently visited by Queen Victoria as a child – and the Monson Colonnade, built to rival the Pantiles. In the Colonnade, as also in Claverley Crescent and elsewhere in the 'new town' Burton made use of cast-iron for the distinctive first floor balconies. The Brighton-based architect, Amon Henry Wilds, was also active in the town during this period, especially in Cumberland Walk.

At Cheltenham spa building reached a peak in 1816 with the opening of the new Assembly Rooms by the Duke of Wellington. It stood on a site in the High Street occupied, since 1900, by a branch of Lloyds' Bank whose directors obviously thought they could not do with it what had already been done with the Montpellier Pump Room and go to the expense of converting the existing building. Its frontage was relatively austere for the early Regency, but within was a magnificent ballroom, spacious card-rooms and an entrance hall 120 feet in length. The ballroom was flanked by Corinthian columns and was to become the focal point of the social life of the spa.

Apart from Joseph Pitt's Pittville Pump Room the New Assembly Rooms were to be Cheltenham's last grand gesture in the spa tradition – notwithstanding the erection of the new Winter Gardens Pavilion in 1876, a glass palace which was demolished by friendly action in 1940. The Winter Gardens Pavilion, although it housed concerts and balls, cannot really be regarded as ever having played a part in Cheltenham's spa story. It came long after the spa was effectively dead and its activities ministered chiefly to residents and to those long-stay visitors who were almost a class of resident in themselves. We may, perhaps, be thankful that the mid-Victorian passion for entertainments in large greenhouses is long spent.

Buxton's main claim to architectural significance for long rested almost solely on its possession of The Crescent. Originally the view toward the Crescent was an open one and, although the opinion may not find acceptance in some quarters, it would probably be to its advantage if many of the trees and shrubs which now clutter the prospect were to be removed. (The same applies to some areas of Georgian Bath).

The two hundred foot curve of The Crescent was designed by John Carr and was to be his only work on a monumental scale. Begun in 1780, it was completed four years later and was primarily intended to house the more wealthy visitors to the spa. William Cavendish, the Fifth Duke of Devonshire, had been something of an *habitué* of Bath and Tunbridge Wells and, well aware of the thermal waters of his native Buxton and of their long medicinal tradition, considered that, if conditions for visitors to the Derbyshire spa could be improved, there was no reason why it should not grow to challenge the spa in the West. He was to invest a considerable amount of his personal fortune in creating the basis of the modern spa-town and, if the Crescent was to be the only large-scale Classical building to be undertaken at Buxton, it was certainly to prove that even one piece of monumental Classical architecture was enough to give an appropriate air of grandeur. The Crescent is now largely occupied by a hotel, but its lines have been tastefully preserved and it remains as much the dominant symbol of Buxton as the Pittville Pavillion is of Cheltenham or the Pantiles are of Tunbridge Wells.

Regency architecture on a minor scale – in terraces and villas – mark almost all the spa towns from Leamington's Lansdowne Crescent and Cheltenham's Combray to Brighton's Kemp Town and Brunswick Town. The cast-iron balconies of the terraces – especially the more individual type to be found particularly in Cheltenham – are as much a hallmark of the Regency architect as the deep friezes and the imposingly projecting cornices which distinguish so many terrace frontages. However, this is not to say that even the Regency terraces, in which we nowadays take such delight, did not suffer from the excursions of the jerrybuilder and the considerations of the cost-conscious, early-nineteenth-century speculator. Many were designed very much with the prime consideration of presenting a good front. The rear of some of the terraces were mean in the extreme – a state of affairs greatly influenced by most of the terraces originally being intended purely for occupation on short leases by a transitory visiting population and not being designed with the interests of permanent residents in mind. Interiors also tended to reflect this preoccupation with visitors and the short-lease.

The relative austerity of design to be found within many a Regency spa terrace house is not there because austere simplicity was the prevailing fashion – in fact the rather ornate interiors of the majority of Regency town-houses proper reveals this to have been very much the opposite of the case – but simply because people occupying premises on a temporary, short-stay basis hardly thought it worthwhile to embellish the interiors further. In fact the Regency terraces of the major spas would, on consideration, be described as being no more than well-fronted hotel rooms – with the extensions beyond this principle accounted for by visitors tending to move *en famille* and to occupy the houses for periods varying anywhere between six months and five years.

Good architects there may have been – and good builders also – but their architecture then, as ever, was limited in achievement by the requirements of the job. In this respect it may be said, that for much of their work in Bath, the Woods were fortunate to enjoy patronage, as did John Forbes and Papworth in the building of their Cheltenham Pump Rooms and Nash in that of the Brighton Pavilion. But – with the exception of the Busby – Wilds combination in Brighton's Kemp Town – the terrace architects and builders were not engaged by patrons who were as interested in architecture for its own aesthetic sake as they were in its functionalism. They were engaged by employers – who wielded the intimidating yard-stick of cost. Given this fact it is hardly surprising that, behind their facades, many Regency terraces were, if not exactly thrown up on the cheap, very much skimped jobs.

Allegations of skimping, however, would hardly have been made in respect of the Brighton terraces of Kemp Town. Brighton's Regency building boom came, as has already been said, rather later than the Regency itself. Amongst other things it was responsible for the creation of the two developments of Brunswick Town and Kemp Town as well as for much of the infilling which was eventually to unite them.

The three architects mostly involved in these creations were Charles Busby and the father and son team of Amon Wilds and Amon Henry Wilds. Busby first arrived in Brighton in 1821, but the Wilds were local men, in so far as the family originated in nearby Lewes and later moved to carry on business based in Brighton. The architectural styles of all three were greatly influenced by John Nash and Decimus

Burton and Busby, in particular, showed great distaste for the earlier formalism of such men as the Adam brothers. Most of their Brighton work was undertaken after Busby had entered into partnership with the two local men.

Kemp Town was the brainchild of Thomas Reade Kemp, M.P. for Lewes, and a wealthy and influential local figure. In many ways he was to be the Brighton counterpart of Cheltenham's Joseph Pitt, for Kemp Town, like Pittville, was something in the nature of a bid for immortality. The project was conceived by the architectural triumvirate on the grand scale and was greatly influenced by Nash's work at such places as London's Regent Street. The original plan was far too ambitious to be ultimately realised. The site was considered too distant from the main centres of social life and the leases of the completed properties were taken up very gradually. Although work began in 1823 by 1834 only thirty-six houses were in fact occupied. The 840-foot sweep of Lewes Crescent had, however, been completed – being 200 feet longer than Bath's Royal Crescent – before Thomas Reade Kemp paid the price of his over-reaching, went bankrupt and had to seek escape from his creditors by flight to France.

Before this happened work had begun on Kemp Town's twin enterprise Brunswick Town, situated in Hove at Brighton's western extremity. Today the two communities have almost merged but, before the arrival of Brunswick Town, Hove had been almost exclusively a small, scattered fishing settlement markedly different from Brighton. After the completion of Brunswick Town Hove retained a separate identity – though the ideal of creating a self-contained new community soon faltered – though now this was largely as a distinct residential development.

Charles Busby was responsible for the larger part of the architecture, working for the estate's owner, the Rev Thomas Scutt. Busby created a more simplified layout for the estate than that which had been followed in Kemp Town. However, this relative austerity was to some degree compensated for by the architectural features being more elaborate. Work began in 1824 and the terraces, Brunswick Town's main features, were completed by 1830. They were marked by their strong

In the early nineteenth century, Bath (above) was still very close to the country—a characteristic which later spa promoters such as Smedley at Matlock Bath (below) took advantage of

The spa at
Scarborough

The Pump Room,
Harrogate

The more domestic architecture of the Royal Crescent, Brighton

The Royal Pavilion, Brighton

The Pantiles, Tunbridge Wells, still well patronised by the Victorians

St Ann's Well, Malvern

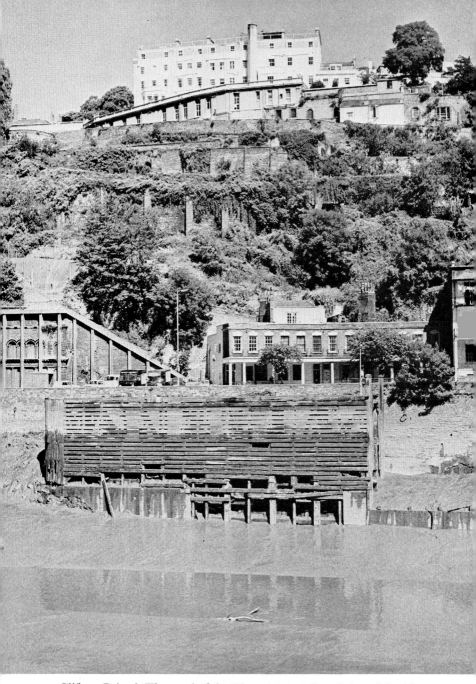

Clifton, Bristol. The mud of the River Avon polluted the original hot well, thus leading to the demise of the spa, but the Grand Spa Hotel, on the top of the hill, contains the Clifton Assembly Rooms dating from the new spa which succeeded the old Hotwells spa

The nineteenth-century 'pepper pot' above the mineral spring
discovered in 1840 at Tenbury Wells, now a café

Modern remnants of the spas (above) The Flask in Flask Walk, Hampstead, London's principal spa, and (below) tasting the waters at Cheltenham

bow fronts, deep friezes and boldly projecting cornices – a style of ornamental work that became increasingly popular after 1830. The supporting Ionic columns also aided the unity of design and Brunswick Square is an exceedingly pleasing example of Charles Busby's work. Nowadays some of the houses are narrower than others – but this is a latter-day departure from Busby's original design, the smaller houses being built at a later date to fill up original gaps. Brunswick Town was designed to be a self-contained community – another parallel with Joseph Pitt's Cheltenham Pittville development. But this element of the project was doomed to failure and the market-hall which Busby built was never fully used for this purpose and was soon to be converted into a school.

Busby and the Wilds were also busy during this period on the infilling between the two developments and to this period belong Marine Square, Eastern Terrace, Bloomsbury Place, Hanover Crescent while, in 1825, Amon Henry Wilds was the architect employed on the Royal Newburgh Assembly Rooms.

But Brighton's major contribution to the architecture of the Regency was the Royal Pavilion. So much time and effort was lavished upon it that, during the course of its construction, the Regent's building activities aroused considerable opposition. He was already deeply in debt and the Pavilion was only possible by increasing his debts still further. In Parliament angry voices were raised that the Prince was mortgaging the future of the Crown and needlessly squandering taxpayers' money. But the Prince was a man of stern resolve. Critics could only be misguided in maligning him. He knew what he wanted and what he wanted he was going to get.

The Pavilion architect was John Nash, who had already made an impact by his work in London. He brought to Brighton not only a design – or, rather, a fusion of designs – that was nothing short of revolutionary, but also new techniques, notably in relation to the new building material of cast-iron. Cast-iron had been used in construction for some years, for bridges and factory roofing and, in domestic building, for balconies, firebacks and external features such as drain-pipes and guttering. But it was Nash who was to incorporate cast-iron into the essential structure of the Royal Pavilion and very many of its features were dependent on his use of the new medium. He was, however, not the first man to use cast-iron in building – 'Iron Jack' Wilkinson had used cast-iron in the construction of some of his works at Broseley, Salop and in a number of houses in the area – but Nash was the first architect to use the new material with such imagination.

The Prince's original Marine Pavilion, the precursor of the Royal Pavilion itself, had been designed by Henry Holland, who had earlier undertaken work for the Prince on his London home of Carlton House. But this soon failed to satisfy the Prince. In 1802 work was begun òn the Royal Stables and Riding House which, surmounted by their dome, may be taken to have marked the beginning of the Royal Pavilion proper. Nash, however, was still to be at work on it in 1822 and its interiors can really be said never to have been completed at all, as the Prince seems to have been continually changing Chinese styles for Indian ones throughout his life.

Building on the grand scale mainly occupied the years 1816-1820 and by then most of the external features of the Oriental palace by the sea were complete, its dome and attendant eastern lines never ceasing to draw comment from visitors – who now seem to have journeyed to Brighton as much to see how the Regent's 'fantastic wonder' was progressing as to take the sea-water cure.

Within, the Pavilion was divided up into a series of semi-public rooms, of which the Chinese seems to have originally have been the most favoured, each furnished, as seemed natural to the Prince, with little regard to cost. The interior, as well as the exterior, was equally the work of John Nash and many of the delicate effects would have been impossible without his cast-iron. Perhaps it seems a little out of place, but Nash, for all his design was not attempting to reproduce a Moorish palace or, come to that, an Oriental Pavilion. The Royal Pavilion, albeit derivative in its inspiration, was created as an original building and, as England was already an industrial nation, it is only natural that Nash should have used the products of that new industry. When Nash had finally completed his interior designs the Prince was to grow tired of them and they were to be endlessly modified during his lifetime.

Apart from the great public functions staged by the Prince, life at the Royal Pavilion was to be relatively quiet – it had its moments, of course, but the Pavilion as a rip-roaring centre of licentious vice is very much an invention of the racier breed of romantic novelist. Surrounded by an intimate circle of friends and mistresses he was content to spend his evenings with small parties gathered around the piano – the Regent, contrary to popular opinion, considered that he was a very good singer. He had a great detestation for affairs of State – especially if they threatened to intrude upon his private life – and more than once the Duke of Wellington had to stay more than one night before the Prince decided he was ready to go through the effort of reading and signing state papers.

But life at the Pavilion was destined to pall and, in the latter years of his kingship, it must have been a sad and desolate place. The Prince was to age rapidly, became increasingly ill and fretful and most of his former friends deserted him. The richness of his surroundings must have seemed to mock his depressed state of mind. Added to this was his increasing unpopularity in the country, especially after the affair of Queen Caroline's divorce. The Pavilion had become an echoing Xanadu and the Prince its ageing and isolated Citizen Kane.

After his death it was to be rarely used as a royal residence and Queen Victoria was one young lady who would never have put foot inside its door, very worried indeed lest the rumoured waywardness of her uncle's life should, in some way, come to contaminate her very soul. Later the Pavilion was bought by Brighton Corporation and today houses – besides a museum – shows, exhibitions and pop concerts. The latter would probably have cheered the old king up.

8

The Cures

For many centuries taking the cure could have better been described as seeking the cure. From earliest times there was some element of sophistication in taking the waters but, throughout the middle-ages and for some time afterward, this was generally limited to journeying to different sites for differing cures and for varying intensity of cure. Few, it seems, were to be liberated from the belief that the powers of medicinal well-waters would be lost if they were not taken *in situ* – a belief that the various well trustees and guardians were in no haste to dispel. Water from some of the more renowned wells was indeed shipped to London and other centres to be sold as elixirs and 'cure-alls' – but local authorities went to considerable pains to point out that these products were almost worthless once they had been removed from their 'life-giving' fountains.

It was to be a far different story in the latter years of the spa-craze. Late Victorian spas were to boast some of the most exotic of 'cures', ranging from Harrogate's mud-baths, to electropathy, compressed-air baths, galvanisation and the host of water-treatments contained in the term hydropathy. Almost all surviving spas at the end of the nineteenth century were to boast that they could provide waters of the mineral composition of most, if not all, of those to be found at the major spas of England and the Continent.

Bathing at well-heads was established far earlier than the general drinking of well-water. At Bath itself, for example, water-drinking caught on very slowly and was not at all general until the beginning of the eighteenth century when the first Pump Room was erected. The majority of the more famous wells of the middle-ages usually rose into a nearby pond or pool and it was the practise for sufferers to immerse themselves up to the neck in the water, often kneeling as if at prayer – as indeed many of them were. In other places where the curative water was not so plentiful, it was the usual practise to bathe only the affected areas such as the eyes or legs.

But the water of some wells was always drunk to some extent. By the end of the sixteenth century the practice was on the increase with doctors, rather than priests, turning to pin their faith on the healing springs.

But, if one was something of a hypochondriac – and many spa-users were more than just something in this direction – and stood in need of cures for a number of different complaints, this could entail a progress approaching the dimensions of a nation-wide Odyssey. The many-sided sufferer would find himself journeying to such varied places as Rotherham for its Eye Well, to Buxton where St Anne's Well would reputedly cure his rheumatism and arthritis, to Malvern's Holy Well to stave off skin-disorders and so on until the whole countryside was covered.

·When these, and other places, later developed as spas this practice of certain wells being patronised for certain disorders naturally persisted – so that we find a large number of what may loosely be termed spa-people, from Daniel Defoe to Sir Edward Bulwer Lytton – forming part of what was almost to become a spa touring-company.

The peripatetic practice began to decline when first Cheltenham, and later Harrogate, developed a complex of wells which contained most of the health-giving minerals. This new practice of concentrating different types of medicinal water at one place perhaps reached its zenith when, in the early years of the present century, Harrogate provided itself with brine-baths using water shipped by rail from the North Sea.

Some spas were to offer a mixture of mineral content in their Pump Rooms – but by the time this was happening the fashion for merely drinking water was already in severe decline.

It was to be superceded by the new science of the

hydropath, who was something of an alien creation as the 'water cure', in this new sense, was largely the child of Vincenz Priestnitz, an Austrian who ran a hydropathic establishment in early nineteenth century Silesia. His most direct English imitators – all of whom were somewhat to modify his rather full-blooded 'cure' – were Drs Gully and Wilson of Malvern, though John Smedley at Matlock and Dr William MacLeod of Yorkshire's Ben Rhydding who also derived much of their inspiration from him.

Gully and Wilson and the rest of the hydropathic league were to rule almost unassailed over the English water-cure until the last quarter of the nineteenth century. By then hydropathy was coming under constant attack as a quack-ridden profession and the hydropaths' defence was not helped by the number of people who were alleged to have died because of the treatment they had been prescribed – it may be said that most died from heart-attacks, not drowning. It was certainly true that a large number of unscrupulous practitioners had entered the hydropath's ranks and it was to be very much a case of 'bad driving out good.'

But, while the public at large became increasingly sceptical about the powers and abilities of the hydropaths, they balanced this by becoming increasingly credulous about water-cures allied to new discoveries in science – many of which were calculated to impress by the use of the sort of grandiose descriptions that were apparently enough to hook the average middle-class Victorian. Victorian quacks tended to use language that was only a small remove from that used by the verbose Music Hall chairman. But the late-Victorian years were the era of 'Progress' and the water-cure had to sound suitably impressive to march along with the spirit of the time.

Hydros began to turn their backs on the mundane and popularly discredited hydropathy in favour of something a little more in tune with a society experiencing what could be said to have been a true 'technological revolution.' So we suddenly discover establishments advertising the beneficial effects of treatments such as faradisation, ergotherapy, electrotherapy and various 'pneumatic' cures. Given that the descriptions of these were sufficiently progressive all were to do well for a time. In our own century their inheritors are the health farms and micro-biotic foods as well as the multiplying number of naturists who have up-dated sun-bathing to the status of heliotherapy.

Bath was one of the first centres to move unconsciously toward hydropathy – and this as early as the late seventeenth century. Besides normal bathing as a treatment in the hot baths there was also the practice of 'bucketing' – in which buckets of hot water would be emptied on those parts of the body considered most in need of treatment. This was later superceded by pumping streams of hot water onto the affected areas – some patients often taking as many as five hundred 'pumps' daily.

On the other hand, the average Bath cure-taker was most expected to benefit merely by the perspiration induced as an after-effect of the bathing.

Most of the spas were later to develop some form of hydropathy as adjuncts to their mineral bathing suites. But it was left for Drs Gully and Wilson to first put hydropathy on a thorough-going footing. In 1842 these two energetic and dedicated men arrived in Malvern in a spirit of being almost the vanguard of a new religion. James Wilson, who had attended Priestnitz's Austrian establishment at Graffenburg, took over the Crown Hotel and renamed it Graffenburg House while Gully built two separate hydropathic enterprises, Tudor House for men and Holyrood House for women.

The hydropaths' basic treatment rested on two different cold-water applications, wet sheeting which involved the patient taking the waters wrapped in wet linen sheets, and the douche which, initially at least, had the patient being deluged with ice-cold water from an over-head pipe whilst he sat naked beneath it. The douche, in this, its most primitive form, was certainly not for either the emotionally or the physically faint-hearted.

Over the years Gully and Wilson and various other hydropaths introduced a number of refinements – perhaps, if they had not done so, they could hardly have expected to stay in business. The rigours of wet-sheeting, the trauma of the douche, up to fifteen Graffenburg glasses of water, a negligible breakfast and daily energetic walking on the hills seems to have been calculated to kill off the English middle-classes rather than restore them to health.

Wet-sheeting had been a basic method of cure at Malvern since medieval times when it had been practised by the monks of Malvern Priory – perhaps, William Langland, author of the narrative poem *Piers Ploughman*, once had to endure the experience. Under Wilson and Gully, however, it was soon to be superceded by the lamp-bath which, in its original form, involved the patient sitting wrapped in coarse blankets on a chair beneath which was positioned the ancestor of the modern camping-stove. It was claimed that this induced sweating to such a degree that a patient could lose pounds within a week. Undeniably many did.

Malvern was soon to offer much more than the lamp-bath. By the mid-1850s hot water treatments had gained an equal footing with the cold water ones, hot air baths were making an appearance in the more avante-garde hydros and vapour baths were well established.

One of Malvern's innovations, the compressed-air bath, was in fact, an importation from Dr William MacLeod's Ben Rhydding. The treatment was recommended largely for asthmatic and bronchial patients but MacLeod also considered it beneficial for those suffering from deafness, chronic migraine and mild tuberculosis. It was at Ben Rhydding – probably while taking MacLeod's rain-bath in which patients sat in a small cubicle while they were sprayed from small jets set into the walls – that John Smedley underwent his sudden conversion to Methodism and the water-cure.

Smedley at first adhered, at his Lea Mills workers' hospital, to almost every aspect of MacLeod's vigorous hydropathic treatment. But his total conversion to MacLeod's water-cure was not to be long-lasting and he was soon to come to the conclusion that the overhead douche was primitive and 'outrageous'. Its abandonment was only one of the many modifications he made to the water-cure treatment.

Smedley was finally to forsake even wet-sheeting – the very

basis of old-style hydropathy – in favour of one involving the use of specially treated bandages. It must be said that these latter-day innovations were largely made when he opened his hydropathic establishment at Matlock – his textile workers had first born the brunt of MacLeod-style treatment.

At his hydro Smedley scaled down the hydropathic treatment and also introduced others to supplement it. Vapour and water baths were provided for selected areas of the body, such as the arms and legs, and considerable use was made of the mustard bath, which was to prove a popular Smedley stand-by for the treatment of rheumatic disorders.

Smedley, however, was a relatively strict hydropathist. It was largely left to others to tinker with and embroider hydropathy to such an extent that the basic treatment was finally submerged in its fringe developments. It was partly this which was to be responsible for its decline. The other overriding reason was the in-rush of opportunists of various kinds into the profession from the mid-1850s onward.

Hydropathy had never succeeded on water alone – in fact, its foremost practitioners had never claimed that it was in itself a cure for any disorder, only a means of alleviating the distress and discomfort already suffered. (Hydropathic cures were claimed mainly by quacks and by patients who genuinely considered that their treatment had ended their complaints). A large part of the hydropaths' success was due, not so much to the water, but to the regime which accompanied it. The hydropaths were against the use of tobacco, snuff, drugs, confectionery and the over-eating which was a mark of middle-class Victorian life. Most of these things were forbidden at the hydros where plain and wholesome food was provided on an adequate, but not generous, scale. It was this policy of general abstinence from the so-called 'good things of life', coupled with an encouragement of energetic exercise – hill walking rather than billiards – that did as much to promote 'the cure' as wet-sheeting and Graffenburg glasses of pure water.

Once this pattern of treatment began to be interfered with the writing was on the wall for the hydropaths – it is not too ambiguous to say that the water-cure was a pure cure which could stand only the minimal amount of impurities before it began to founder.

The change began most markedly at Malvern, which, despite the fact that hydros had been established in many other parts of the country, was generally regarded as the centre of the hydropathic business. Gully and Wilson were still firmly entrenched as its leading practitioners, but many less dedicated men had now moved in to set up practice and to trade upon their reputation. Well aware that Gully and Wilson had virtually cornered the true hydropathic trade for themselves the new arrivals had to resort to gimmicks to attract their clients. Dr Grindrod and his compressed-air bath was not too far removed from the respectable hydropathic tradition – but when someone calling himself a 'Medical Mesmerist and Magneto Electrician' set himself up in business nearby it was a doom-ridden pointer of the way things were destined to go.

One reason why hydropathy began to go such strange and fatal ways was that – like the more established medical profession of the time – it was run by men who had to be both hydropaths and businessmen. Gully and Wilson, and their more respectable imitators, were hydropaths first and businessmen second. Many of their later rivals were to be businessmen first and hydropaths hardly at all.

The new men took the view that 'they all had a living to make' and, perhaps, while the old hydropaths could afford to be high-minded they were in no such fortunate position. From the start Gully and Wilson had imposed a strict discipline on their patients. It had been accepted partly because the people they had attracted had been high-minded enough themselves, in relation to their own health, to go along with anything that would appear to promote their ultimate well-being. But then Gully and Wilson had undoubtedly taken the cream of the sufferers, people such as Wordsworth, Darwin, Florence Nightingale and Dickens who had enough self-discipline of their own to be able to accept that asked of them by the hydropaths.

The new men therefore faced two problems. Their patients formed a second strata beneath the august patrons of the established hydros and secondly they had to compete with Gully and Wilson and to compete they had to claim to be better. In many cases better was actually to mean worse.

In their efforts to attract and keep patients many hydropaths ceased to insist on the disciplines that had habitually accompanied the hydropathic cure. A number of establishments gave way on the no-smoking rule and, because of the complaints of wealthy patients, the fare offered at some hydros was soon found to be rivalling that to be obtained at the leading hotels. At Ben Rhydding Dr MacLeod bowed to patients' pressure and rescinded the no-alcohol rule. At Malvern some of the newer establishments were to begin life with alcohol freely permitted – and actually incorporated into the cure, various wines and spirits now being considered to assist patients suffering from certain disorders.

The use of alcohol, however, was a clear departure from hydropathic principles. But then so was the use of drugs, and electropathy and other treatments which smacked vaguely of the 'Black Arts'. Commercial exploitation also showed up when Lea and Perrins – the manufacturers of Worcester sauce – arrived in Malvern to take over the Holy Well with a bottling plant manufacturing 'Malvern Seltzer Water'. This was later replaced by a plant belonging to Schweppes.

All this tinkering with the purity of the original cure was bound to bring it into eventual disrepute. Some of the more established hydropaths, such as Gully and Grindrod, recognised this and wrote articles deploring the current trends. But articles were powerless to put matters right even if they did succeed in making the standpoint of their individual writers clear.

It could almost be said that hydropathy fell into a decline on a class basis. The high-minded intellectuals and aristocrats who had formed the basic clientèle of the earlier hydropaths came to be outnumbered by the new rich who were taking the cure at the hydros for roughly the same reasons that their predecessors in the previous century had taken the waters of Bath, Cheltenham and Tunbridge – namely because the leaders of mid-Victorian society had made it fashionable.

The prescription for energetic exercise also ceased to be

made out by many of the new 'commercial' hydropaths – so that what had constituted a large element of the cure was now effectively abandoned. This was a departure from a principle which had been followed even in the days of the earliest spas, when the provision of 'walks' between and around various well-heads had been one of the first considerations of spa-promoters.

With hydropathy now being increasingly divorced from the fringe regime which surrounded the actual water-cure – a fringe regime which, when added up, was possible more than 50% of the total cure – and with its hydropathic content being, let us say, considerably diluted by new and less tried forms of treatment, it may be said that in many of the newer hydropathic establishments hydropathy was really non-existent.

But, in mid-Victorian England, it was difficult to draw such distinctions between genuine hydropathy and its gimmick-ridden associates. The conventional medical world had always looked askance at the water-practitioners – perhaps with rather envious eyes, as they had often succeeded where more orthodox treatment had lamentably failed. In general many medical men were only too willing to lump both the genuine and quack-commercial hydropaths together and, by publicising the excesses of opportunists, effectively to discredit the genuinely dedicated.

Such anti-hydropathic campaigns as were now launched by the *Lancet* and other medical journals may not have met with much success in earlier years. But the climate of opinion amongst the hydropaths' new public was now swinging against them and the campaign met with considerable popular support. Many were disappointed that the cure had not lived up to their expectations. After attending one of the newer hydros they had been surprised to discover that, after a round of heavy meals, heavy drinking, tempered only a little by the occasional hot bath and the casual game of billiards, they had not experienced any great improvement to their health. If they had attended one of the hydros which also permitted the liberal use of Victorian medicines they would probably have found that, far from improving, their health would have literally deteriorated.

Even those who had attended establishments run on the most strict of hydropathic lines would probably have found something to complain about. The point here was that the true hydropathic cure took time – it was not something that could be expected to achieve much good in a mere fortnight. It was a long job. The earlier patients had been prepared to spend up to two or three months at a hydro and then, most likely, go on to another. Some would even follow this up by a visit to Continental spas and would return to their original cure centre the following year. Thus the 'cure', taken in this prolonged way, was something in the nature of a sabbatical year, and was really only to be fully indulged by the wealthy. Some practitioners did realise this and issued books which detailed how the patient might practise follow-up treatment in his own home.

However, if hydropathy was basically a long-term treatment it largely failed to come over as such to many of its later and fickle public. Various publications were issued by eminent men extolling the benefits of the cure. It was these that made the greatest claims for hydropathy – not the hydropaths themselves – and it was from these that the general public appears to have come to the conclusion that a couple of weeks in a hydro would see an instant end to all their ills.

The hydropaths' mid-Victorian patients were largely members of the new bourgeoisie – flocking to the hydros partly because they considered it the fashionable thing to do, partly to be cured as quickly as possible and at the least inconvenience to themselves. From their point of view speed was the essence. It had to be; they might be the new rich, but they were certainly not rich enough to be able to afford to undertake the cure for up to three months and certainly could not follow it up with a journey to some Continental centre. The result was that they expected too much too quickly and, when this was coupled to the fact that the hydro they attended had probably practically abandoned almost all the fringe hydropathic principles, they could really expect none other than disappointment.

These two factors – adverse medical opinion and a

disappointed public – combined to bring the whole practice of hydropathy into disrepute. A few steadfast practitioners remained in the field, supported by a sufficient number of steadfast patients. But the quacks were driven from it, together with a large number of hydropaths whose only fault that they had called their treatment by the same name as that used by their less reputable rivals.

The water religion had been found wanting and was now to give rise to a host of new sects, most of which included some form of hydropathy as a fringe exercise. Malvern's 'Medical Mesmerist and Magneto Electrician' was only one of the earlier examples of men who were to advertise treatments that sounded like something proclaimed as a fair-ground side-show.

Other treatments were, perhaps, more genuinely inspired – including electrotherapy which had, as one of its many forms, the electrical treatment of patients while immersed in a hot bath. It was not recommended for children or those of weak constitution – and even those of strong constitution may afterwards have had their doubts about it. Electrotherapy was practised at Malvern, Matlock and a number of other places and, in modern form, still survives at Harrogate.

Electrotherapy was claimed to be good for rheumatics, arthritics and, amongst many others, for those suffering from gastric disorders. A more refined extension of the treatment passed under the name of ergotherapy. In this treatment electrical impulses were directed to various parts of the body to stimulate muscular reaction. It was claimed that this was of great benefit to those patients whose treatment required exercise but who were too weak to be able to undertake it. Other forms of electropathy were practised, notably faradisation and galvanism. Galvanism involved the passing of an electric current through the patient's body via an attendant-electrician – there were to be no electrical doctors – who was first instructed to try the strength of the current applied upon himself. Galvanisation was considered to tone up the whole body and nervous system – and the resident electrician must have been the most toned-up man in many a hydro. Faradisation came in many forms, but the most general was for a patient to sit with his feet against a large electrode while the attendant passed the other electrode about various parts of his body, there being different ways of treating various areas. It must all have been a rather invigorating experience – though electropathy, in all its forms, was not the only treatment on offer in the modern, late-Victorian hydro.

Various other treatments were now available and were lumped together in the larger hydros' Inhalatoria. As the word indicates these treatments were linked by the fact that they all involved inhaling. The claims for this method of treatment rested on the premise that beneficial vapours and gases were more effective than the customary drugs as they by-passed what could be an over-strained stomach and were directed more expeditiously to the seat of the disorder. The principles involved probably were of great use to the asthematic and bronchial – but it attracted many who suffered from no more than laryngitis, actors, singers and clergymen forming a considerable portion of its devotees.

But the great cure – which bid fair to surplant hydropathy completely at many of the treatment centres – was radium – radiation which, at the turn of the century, was still very much an unknown quantity.

This did not deter many resorts declaring, to all and sundry, the beneficial properties of their own brand of radioactivity. It was not applied directly – seeing that no one could precisely locate it this was hardly possible – but was said to be in both the air and waters of certain spas. Bath and Buxton were amongst the towns which claimed that their waters were particularly endowed with the newly discovered element.

The major surviving spas of the Edwardian period, Harrogate, Llandrindod and Buxton were still in fitful business as cure-centres largely because they judiciously catered for all tastes amongst the 'cure'-public. Mineral water drinking and bathing survived in the Pump Rooms and bathing suites which offered all manner of mixtures of the old cures, hydropathy, electropathy in all, its varied forms, inhaling rooms and emanatoria, plus various treatments offered by men who were the direct descendants of Malvern's

'Medical Mesmerist and Magneto Electrican'. There was a strange mixture of science and pretention which catered more than adequately for the varied public which still flocked to the inland centres, like their predecessors for more than three centuries, in search of the 'cure'.

9

The Social Round

It was the Romans – who built Britain's first public baths – who were first to endow taking the waters with a sense of social occasion. To them the great baths of Aquae Sulis, and the lesser ones of Buxton and, perhaps, Ilkley and Droitwich, were far more than places where one just went to become cured. They were social centres on a par with the Forum and the Amphitheatre.

Aquae Sulis mixed commerce, music, poetry, medicine and politics with its curative waters. It was a spa in the true sense of the word, attracting customers from all over Britain and the Northern Provinces of the Empire. The baths were meeting places where, if the experience of more recent spas is anything to go by, the latest scandals were spread, the latest political intrigues begun, and where deals were reached over everything ranging from the sale of wine and corn to who should be the next Governor of the province.

Masseurs, physicians and barbers plied their trade around the baths, as did the wine-sellers, musicians and pimps and procurers who catered for every known form of vice. Aquae Sulis was a mecca for the legionary officer, wearied by the lonely command of some distant frontier garrison, for the businessman wishing to get away from the cut-throat atmosphere of the provincial capital, for the administrative officer frustrated by imperial red-tape, for the provincial big-fish who were wealthy in Britain but who would have cut a very meagre dash amid the splendours of imperial Rome, and for every species of hanger-on who wished to ensure that a little of Britain's new found prosperity strayed toward their own pockets.

Roman Britain was a slave-based society and Aquae Sulis'

baths depended very largely on slaves for their functioning. It was, in many ways, not such a radically different situation to that encountered in the Bath of the late seventeenth and early eighteenth centuries. As Celia Fiennes was to imply, an economic serfdom was almost as efficient as slavery in ensuring that the lower orders did not stray too far out of their place. In fact very little was to change and, as the baths became increasingly the resort of elegant and aristocratic society, it was a near-Roman regime that came to be re-instated – something emphasized by the most brilliant flowering of the Bath of Beau Nash being in the very midst of the Augustan age, when England looked back to imperial Rome for so much of its artistic inspiration. In fact, in eighteenth-century, hedonistic Bath the only marked thing that differentiated this period of nominal Christian luxury from its Roman predecessor would appear to have been the absence of the young boy attendants in which so many of the elder male clientèle had, following their Greek cultural mentors in this direction, taken such attentive delight. Strange things did go on in the warm waters of eighteenth-century Bath, but Christian morality had at least succeeded in removing young boys to more chaste climes, or at any rate to church choirs where their temptations were reserved to be the test of many an Augustan clergyman. But, if this element of the 'cure' of Roman times was to be absent from the immediate environs of eighteenth-century Bath's crowded thermal waters, then the fashionable equivalent of almost all others was certainly to be present.

The satirist Ned Ward in his "A Step to Bath" gives a startling, if somewhat exaggerated, account of the standards of general behaviour at the Cross Bath – the most popular of Bath's public baths – which would seem to indicate that public bathing habits are perhaps, immune from change:

Here is performed all the wanton dalliance imaginable; celebrated beauties, panting breasts and curious shapes, almost exposed to public view; languishing eyes, darting killing glances, tempting amorous postures, attended by soft music, enough to provoke a vestal to forbidden pleasure, captivate a saint and charm a Jove. The vigorous sparks present the ladies with several antick postures, as sailing on their backs, then embracing the element, sink in a rapture and by accidental design thrust an outstretched arm; but where the water concealed, so ought my pen. The spectators in the galleries please their roving fancies with this lady's face, another's eyes, a third's heavy breasts and profound air. In one corner stood an old lecher whose years bespoke him no less than three-score and ten, making love to a young lady not exceeding fourteen.

Although Ward was, to some extent, indulging in satirical license, it is quite clear from this and other contemporary accounts, that Bath at the beginning of the eighteenth century was still very much an untamed place. Ward's account was written some five years before Richard Nash first arrived in the city and may be taken, cautiously, as some indication of the general conduct of the baths for the preceeding century.

Viewed by modern standards the general condition of seventeenth-century Bath had been deplorable – but then, the same could be said in relation to almost any English town of the time. Conditions at Bath, however, were to be increasingly aggravated by the growing annual inflow of visitors, especially following the Restoration and the visits of the Court. Like most towns of the period Bath was still essentially a medieval place, its streets narrow and unpaved with sanitary arrangements of the most rudimentary nature, houses that were fire- and health-risks combined, non-existent street-lighting, a lack of general order, with it being necessary for most of the population to walk the streets armed in case of attack.

The town was still prosperous on the basis of its connection with England's old staple industry, the wool-trade. But this, especially in the West Country, had been in progressive decline since before the outbreak of the Civil War and, by the beginning of the eighteenth century, it had become evident that it would never revive in the area to the extent of its former importance. Accordingly the burgesses began to cast around for something to take its place as the corner-stone of the town's prosperity. The increasing spa trade saw their interests quickened in creating Bath as a health and pleasure centre – but the general medieval character of the town presented many problems. There had to be development – and much of it – before Bath could really be said to be ready to attract the 'right people'. But the burgesses were willing to do something themselves and, in co-operation with Richard Nash, were to be responsible for a municipal 'clean-up' campaign that resulted in the paving of some of the more important thoroughfares, the creation of closed as against the traditional open sewers and the provision of rudimentary forms of street lighting. But it was Richard Nash himself, through his various subscription lists, who was, to a considerable degree, responsible for Bath gradually acquiring both a sense of order and taste. He created, within the spa, an aura of social refinement which was to compliment the Classical movement in architecture and the arts at large which was later to give to the Augustan Age the associated tag of 'The Age of Elegance'. It was, however, an uphill struggle.

At Tunbridge Wells the situation was somewhat different. Here, when the waters had first been discovered at the beginning of the seventeenth century, there had been no medieval town, but the smallest of rural settlements. Because of the lack of accommodation the first royal visitors were housed in temporary accomodation and it was not until the latter decades of the seventeenth century that there were sufficient buildings to house the more important water-takers. Even then, many had still to seek accommodation in neighbouring towns.

Not being a town, like Bath, with a large indigenous population, Tunbridge was to develop along very different lines. From the start it was essentially a tourist resort with its population expanding to meet the gradually increasing number of fashionable visitors. As such it did not have to face Bath's problems of having to impose a social order upon a population essentially unused to anything but the most basic of economic disciplines. From the first the Court was to provide the model for social life – though, as this was the frivolous and libertine court of Charles II, this was hardly to be the most taxing of disciplines. At a later stage the spa was largely to be taken over by Richard Nash himself. But the imposition of Nash's 'Rules of Conduct' was to come at a point when Tunbridge was already in decline in relation to Bath and when the influence of the Court had been largely removed.

Late seventeenth-century Tunbridge, of course, did not possess, as did Bath, medieval thermal baths. It was a cold water cure centre with waters reputed to cure a host of complaints, including infertility which latter complaint seems to have been a particular affliction of Stuart queens for it was to bring, in steady succession, Charles I's Henrietta Maria, Charles II's Catherine of Braganza and, in her own right, Queen Anne.

By the time of Anne's visit a social routine had been well developed. The buildings of the new town were now catering almost exclusively for the spa-trade, with assembly rooms, coffee-houses, gaming rooms. The Pantiles – though not yet paved – were already in existence as the Upper and Lower Walks and there were numerous shops and lodging houses as well as a number of bowling greens – bowls, in popularity, being something like the Restoration equivalent of present-day soccer.

As at Bath the waters tended to be taken early in the day with the rest of the time being taken up with social pastimes of one sort or another. The round of the coffee-houses and the assembly rooms could be a rather dull one and, as at Bath, one's enjoyment was entirely dependent upon the company. This, however, was not lacking and differed little from that of Bath and tended to include most of the same people. The society of the spas, however, was far more accessible than that of London. Etiquette did exist, but in a much modified form and much of the spa's popularity with the bourgeoisie is accounted for by them here being able to hob-nob with the nobility and fashionable almost on terms of equal footing – something that would have been quite impossible in the comparatively rigid stratifications of London society.

Nevertheless, too great an intermingling of the classes was rightly considered to have its dangers, especially in Bath were the local squirearchy could be calculated not to mix with ease with the relative sophisticates from London. At the beginning of the eighteenth century Bath was something of a social tinder-box. Almost everyone carried a sword, not only in the street but also in the ballroom (something which, however, was common to early eighteenth-century society in general) the manner of the visitors veered between the most elegant and the most coarse, duels were commonplace as was fighting between the 'gentlemen' and the sedan-chair operators who would cudgel their way into battle armed with the staves of their chairs. In fact the elegance was surrounded – almost drowned – by the ambience of a Wild West frontier town. If Beau Nash had not designed and imposed his social system on the spa there is every reason to believe that someone else must have undertaken the task. Bath, without some form of social regulation at this time, would have found it almost impossible to survive as a spa.

Nash's social regime at Bath was to be explained and justified by Oliver Goldsmith in his 'Life of Richard Nash'. He is at pains to deal with the influx of the new bourgeoisie.

"Regularity repressed pride," he maintained, "and, that lessened, people of fortune became fit for society. Though ceremony is very different from politeness, no country was ever yet polite that was not first ceremonious. The natural gradation of breeding begins in savage disgust, proceeding to indifference, improves by attention, by degrees refines into ceremonious observance, and the trouble of being ceremonious at length produces politeness, elegance and ease."

In fact Goldsmith here was writing what may be called a latter-day prospectus for the "national finishing school" Bath was to become.

It was not Richard Nash who laid down the basic regime of the Bath water-takers – that, to some degree, had existed before he arrived at the town. But, by means of the subscription lists intended to augment the spa's social facilities, he quickly elevated himself to the position of being its general social overseer. The spa waters had soon been relegated to a very inferior place in the list of Bath's attractions and, as Goldsmith pointed out, the gaming tables drew more custom than the baths themselves. It was largely the influence of Nash which prevented the gaming rooms from becoming particularly bloody 'cathedrals of chance', – though he was never to succeed in stamping out duelling in the town completely. His insistence on rules of general behaviour in the Assembly Rooms also prevented the balls from being something in the order of a competition between the barn-dance and the quadrille. Ladies were not admitted to the floor in aprons or outdoor habits – something of which duchesses no less than merchant's wives were occasionally to be found guilty – nor were gentlemen admitted in riding boots or wearing swords – the last restriction being waived for members if the military. By the time that the average local squire or the East India Company merchant had spent a month or two at Bath he would, according to Nash, have learnt how to temper his moneyed arrogance and to secure admission to fashionable society anywhere. As one of the town's local historians was later to point out – one of Nash's most important contributions to the smooth-running of the town was that he created "a ready-made programme that relieved the pleasure-seekers from the strain of invention and finally the decorum and ceremony that invested frivolous pastimes with an imaginary dignity".

By the 1740s, for reasons already mentioned in an earlier chapter, Nash's influence at Bath was on the wane. Yet, in 1742, appeared his Rules of Conduct which were posted in the Pump Room and were not only to have an influence on Bath but on almost all other English spas as well.

The Rules of Conduct were an attempt to impose a social discipline within a velvet glove. Their tone was not one of command, rather of snobbish persuasion. The following give some indication of their style:

That gentlemen of fashion never appearing in a morning before ladies in caps or gowns show breeding and respect.
That no gentleman give his tickets for balls to any but gentlewomen NB unless he has none of his acquaintance
That no gentleman or lady takes it ill that another dances before them – except such as have no pretence to dance at all.
That the older ladies and children be content with a second bench at the ball, as being past or not yet come to perfection.
That a visit of ceremony at coming to Bath, and another at going

away, is all that is expected of ladies of quality and fashion;
except impertinents.

That no person take it ill that anyone goes to another's play, or
breakfast, and not theirs – except captious by nature.

That all whisperers of scandal and lies be taken for their authors.

These were not 'rules' in the strict sense, but rather social
advice. Nevertheless, the advice was ignored at peril and it
was this creation of convention that was to be Nash's greatest
legacy not only to Bath, but to all the earlier spas. In the early
nineteenth century the Master of Ceremonies at Margate was
pronouncing 'Rules of Conduct' for the new resort closely
modelled on those of Bath. At the Margate Assembly Rooms
it was laid down that the dancing was to begin at 8.00 p.m.
and end at 12 midnight "precisely". Nash's 'Rules of
Conduct' were, in fact, to be used without modification at
Tunbridge and with only slight alteration at Cheltenham,
Brighton, Leamington, Margate and most of the southern and
Midland spas.

As the years wore on, however, the purposes of the 'Rules'
were to undergo a change which was at direct variance with
Nash's original intentions in framing them. Rather than being
interpreted as something in the way of a cautionary social
education they now became a tool to impose the evolving
social exclusiveness of the spas. At first exclusiveness had been
maintained almost solely by distance and local pricing. In
days when it cost a small fortune to transport one's self, family
and baggage over miry, virtually non-existent roads (and even
the journey from Tunbridge to London could take a couple of
days) it was hardly worth making the effort, even if the
potential visitor could afford it, unless the stay was to be a
relatively long one. Up to the latter decades of the eighteenth
century distance certainly *was* some object in England and the
exclusiveness of the spas was effectively maintained without
recourse to any more direct methods.

The creation of John Palmer's 'mail-coach revolution'
began to put an end to this state of affairs. The Bath road
became one of the fastest in the country, Tunbridge became a
matter of hours from London and most of the other spas found

themselves suddenly opened up to people who would have been excellent fodder for the 'national finishing schools' if they had still been functioning along these lines. But they were not – and largely because Richard Nash had done his job so well. By the end of the eighteenth century 'polite society' had already been created, and its creation was very much due to the earlier influence of Nash, his successors and imitators. It was a mobile, interlocking society functioning very much on a network basis. Nash had performed his job to a point even beyond his own expectations for, on the basis of a social code, he had civilised the upper reaches of the English social spectrum – yet, at the same time, this society had produced a brittle elegance which came to be exercised as a barrier against the uninitiated. The spas ceased to be 'finishing schools'. Elegant society was a visible creation and regarded itself as an exclusive preserve and, from an internal point of view, it was finished beyond anything but self-perpetuation.

Of course English society did not completely stratify – there were enough influential people around who could see the dangers inherent in such a situation. Social mobility still functioned on a basis of money, something which had been evident since at least Tudor times, and Ralph Allen's rise to fame and fortune is only one of the more spectacular examples of the age. But it was, to a considerable extent, the grisly spectacle of the French Revolution that kept English society from becoming excessively rigid. True, Tory politicians who had, with brief lapses, been pursuing a policy of strengthening the power of the Crown, were initially to act repressively, but Whig politicians such as Fox and the popular 'Radical' Jack Wilkes were voices which could not be entirely ignored. In Cheltenham, for example, the Whig, Colonel Berkeley, was the champion of the small farmer and the shopkeeper, people who the Whig nobility saw as the basis of their popular power in their contest with the patronage-supported Tories. In fact, though Cheltenham was to be long-considered a Tory stronghold, it was to return Whig/Liberal members to Parliament for many years.

But, despite the popular stance of Whig politicians, both Whig and Tory leaders came very largely from the same class of landed proprietors, and when they came to the spas they were very much off-duty. From the point of view of William Cobbett – a Radical of humbler origins than most of his Whig associates – Cheltenham's seasonal society existed almost solely to squander ill-gotten gains and to bring about an expansion of the town which would gobble-up the countryside – from Cobbett's standpoint, the traditional basis of England's wealth. It was from the bias of this reasoning that Cobbett was to dub the town the 'Devouring Wen' and did not scruple to declare his satisfaction when he discovered that Joseph Pitt's Pittville development was running into disaster.

In 1816 Arthur Wellesley, Duke of Wellington, came to the town and Cheltenham went *en fête*, even though the 'close run thing' had been a year earlier and the Duke was now bogged down in Continental goodwill visits and the interminable Congress of Vienna. On such occasions the 'new and improved' Rules were brought into operation with determination, particularly at the spa's new Assembly Rooms which the Duke opened with an especially lustrous ball on 29th July. Here it was circulated that "no clerk, hired or otherwise in this town or neighbourhood" could gain admittance, as well as "no person concerned in retail trade; no theatrical or other public performers by profession" – the latter exclusion probably being something which at least Mrs Jordan, with her close connection with the Regent, could probably have side-stepped. The town guide-book, which Simon Moreau had started some thirty years before and which was now under the superintendance of Alexander Fotheringham – who had succeeded James King as Master of Ceremonies only a few weeks earlier – declared that new visitors to the spa would be advised to obtain "a letter of introduction from their friends, who may have previously resided here, or may be acquainted with the resident or visiting families of the town" in order to gain admittance to the new rooms.

This was only the first hurdle. Dress was specifically regulated and prohibition from the ballroom was applied to any "gentleman in boots or half-boots except officers in navy or army uniform; and undress trowsers or coloured pantaloons cannot be permitted on any account". Women were, if anything, even more rigorously censored and the various promulgations efficiently ensured that the retail trader – toward whom established society at the Midland spas seems to have had an unusual aversion – certainly did not succeed in entering this particular preserve of polite society.

This latter development toward social exclusiveness was one reason for many inland spas failing as they did in face of the late Regency drift to the coast. When high society packed its bags to desert Bath, Cheltenham and Leamington there was no remaining hard-core of middle-class visitors to take their place. The Masters of Ceremonies had drawn the circle of exclusiveness so tightly around the old centres that, in the end, it strangled them.

At the coastal spas visitors poured in over good roads and on ships that plied daily from the capital. The Masters of Ceremonies and 'assembly-room society' in general were besieged by a host of day-trippers. When the host expanded to a horde both the Masters of Ceremonies and polite society decamped either to places which retained a precarious exclusiveness by price or to take refuge at the more distant English resorts or those of the Continent. The coastal resorts, like most of the inland spas, became, rather than aristocratic strongholds, the bastions of the new middle-class. The inland spas became their residences, the coastal spas their pleasure grounds. It was, in the light of the times, a triumph of democracy but, at the same time, a cultural disaster.

From Cheltenham and its social allies not only had libertinism and wanton dalliance been banished; so had patronage. The middle-class took over the vacated towns in a far different spirit, one which lacked the ebullience of the aristocratic Regency and was endowed, instead, with a near-modern sobriety. Not for the spa's new residents and visitors the ideal which had lain behind the creation of the Classical Bath of the Woods. Theirs was not the tradition of the landed estate, of the country house, of elegance mingled with a pastoral landscape – for them, the creation of *rus in urbe* was not just irrelevant, it was psychologically impossible. England's new wealth came now, not from the land, but from expanding industry. Its new bourgeoisie were not the sons of Cirencester farming-stock, as had been Cheltenham's Joseph Pitt, but of men who had risen in industry in the new, smoke-belching towns of industrial England. Their tradition was almost wholly urban and it was to be an urban landscape and an urban pattern of living which they were to impose upon the spas of the Victorian age.

Socially the calling-card came to replace the Master of Ceremonies, as what remained of spa society broke up into numerous segments. The private gathering was already a dominant social feature, according to Jane Austen, in the Bath of the Regency. By the end of the period it had become a way of life, at least at most of the inland spas. Middle-class society tended to by-pass the Assembly Rooms in favour of large houses. The regimes at the newer health centres, such as Matlock and Malvern were, at first, inimicable even to this. But, when they eventually relaxed, it was the large hotel that here tended to perform the functions of the private residence.

Acceptable Victorian middle-class society was of the withdrawing kind – it did not believe over much in ostentation, it frowned on the theatre, distrusted both the lower and the upper classes, believed in Toryism of the Evangelical stamp and practised a formal sobriety of which the Temperence Leagues were only the most obvious and extreme manifestations. Its ultimate receptical was the withdrawing room, and it was drawing room society that henceforth was to dominate the spas as it did most of the rest of Victorian society. The upper-class regarded it all with distaste, but they too had retreated to their houses and, while the country-house party dictated the affairs of England it was the drawing-room which was to dictate its essential social pattern.

This exclusiveness was to be found operating in the early years of the nineteenth century at some of the declining spas and was to be general at all those that remained in business at the end of the century. The comforts of the drawing room was very much what the average spa hotel or latter-day hydro aimed to give its patrons. At Matlock, for instance, hotel drawing-rooms were decked out with wicker furniture, views of the surrounding countryside, while the library offered volumes of local history and romance usually headed by Scott's *Peveril of the Peak*. The large hotels organised balls and concerts of their own – so that the position of Master of Ceremonies, if retained, was very much that of an unnecessary social embellishment. On the public side the spas were to become drabber places than they had been in their Regency bloom. The Regency passion for spectacle, for illuminations, firework displays, pageants and the like was not so freely indulged simply because there were not enough people with money and the inclination to indulge it. The Victorian spas tended to be conducted as businessess, not as social playgrounds. Smedley's hydro was a somewhat typical expression of the mood, for it was said that he designed the building at Matlock so that, should the spa boom fade, he would easily be able to convert it into a textile mill. Not for John Smedley and his kind were the Classical Temples to Hygenia that dotted the older spas. What was required was something solid and respectable – buildings that would breed confidence and which would not make the new patrons feel out of their element by being rooted in a tradition in which they had no part.

The development of the coastal resorts was somewhat different and, to a certain extent, they avoided the latter-day stuffiness of most of the surviving inland spas. Masters of Ceremonies they certainly had, such as Robinson Farside, who ruled over Scarborough in the latter decades of the eighteenth century. Farside was concerned so it would seem, not so much with the social niceties but with economic realities. The balls at the Long Room at Scarborough had to pay and Farside's list of Rules was framed with little else than this consideration in mind.

RULES FOR THE LONG-ROOMS AT SCARBORO'

I.   That every subscriber pay for the room and lights 10s.6d.

II.   That there be one dress ball, and two undress nights at each room every week.

RULES FOR THE BALL NIGHTS

I.   That every subscriber may either subscribe half a guinea for the season, or pay 1s. 6d. admittance every ball-night, for which they will be entitled to tea – this optional.
II. That all gentlemen who dance country dance, pay 2s. for the music.
III. That every person who calls for cakes, negus, &c. pay for the same.
IV. NONSUBSCRIBERS pay 5s. admittance.

RULES FOR UNDRESS NIGHTS

I.   That every person who drinks tea pays 1s.
II. That all gentlemen who dance, pay 2s. for the music.
III. EVERY person who calls for cakes negus, Xc. pay for the same.
IV. NONSUBSCRIBERS to pay 2s. admittance, and subject to the above the rules.

Judging from the above there obviously wasn't much of the Beau Nash about Robinson Farside. It should be pointed out that negus was a fashionable drink made of wine, hot water, sugar, lemon and nutmeg.

Social life here revolved around the Assembly Rooms, the theatre, circulating libraries, the shops and the Pump Room. But Scarborough was developing as a sea-bathing resort as early as the 1720s and, by the end of the century, sea-bathing and sea-drinking had largely replaced the daily glasses in the Pump Room. Bathing machines covered the foreshore and just as many bathers as those who used the machines preferred to enter naked from the water's edge. But Scarborough remained 'fashionable', easily outclassing its nearby rivals of Redcar and Bridlington. In Victorian times no coastal resort in the North would surpass it for its air of grandeur and opulence.

The South-Coast resorts, of course, went down before the invasion of the railway day-tripper whose needs for cheap enjoyment, cheap food and even cheaper thrills radically changed the old resorts beyond all but architectural recognition. London-beside-the-sea took over Southend, Margate, Ramsgate and Brighton by the mid-1860s just as

Wakes Week, Lancashire was to take over the resorts of the
North West coast. The coastal resorts were drowned in their
own popularity and what fashionable social life there was
amongst the residents took place at the level of a barely visible
sub-strata.

Harrogate, of course, was rather different, largely because it
did not go into retreat like so many spas, but actively
expanded its activities throughout the Victorian era. It
survived until the end of the Edwardian period as what was,
apparently, the last representative of the spirit of the old
Regency spa. But it is to be doubted if the Prince would have
felt at home there.

Unlike the Prince's Pavilion, the Harrogate Kursaal and its
Winter Gardens were not the product of royal caprice, which
had somehow come to be developed as one of the most
curious, and at the same time, elegant buildings of their age.
They were not, like Cheltenham's Pittville or Montpellier
Pump Room, the happy accident of an alliance between
speculative building and an architectural tradition which had
been maturing for well over a century. They were, instead, the
product of municipal enterprise, engineered rather than
designed and Gothic in more than one sense in that their
inspiration was not to be sought in any English tradition but
in the success story of the German spas. Yet Harrogate is
hardly to be blamed for this for, though its roots were firmly
embedded in the general development of the English spa, it
was a late flower of the European, rather than the English
variety.

The presence of so much royalty helped to make the
Harrogate season rather a glittering affair – but it was
essentially a summer extension of the London Season and was
conducted in much the same manner. Balls took place in the
public rooms – from which the general public was very much
excluded – or in the more spacious hotels – to which they
could not gain admittance. Nevertheless, the presence of
people such as Edward VII and the Russian Tzarina helped to
give the town an aura of somewhat ponderous regality, an
atmosphere well suited to nourish Europe's peripatetic royal
cousins.

But the off-duty pomp vanished overnight with the outbreak of the First World War and Harrogate celebrated national feeling by the renaming of its Kursaal as the Royal Hall. It would be true to say that Harrogate did not exactly reel under the impact of this latest of England's long line of Continental wars. Initially the spa seems actually to have prospered. But such a blood-letting and such a profound dislocation of England's established social pattern was to have its effect on the spa – and those others still in business – during the early twenties. What the Great War began, the proliferation of patent medicines continued and the effects of the Depression taken with both, spoke disaster for the remaining spas.

By 1939 Harrogate's spa functions had severely contracted and even the 1920s Winter Garden Palm Court recitals began to appear as something of a golden age. Other spas had already been driven out of business and Harrogate may have counted itself fortunate to have survived at all. It was, however, soon destined to join them and the last remnants of the social round of the old spas was not to survive the entry of Harrogate – the faded queen of the Edwardian Age – into the Second World War.

10

The School Towns

As the rot began to set in for many of the inland spa towns – at points ranging from the third decade of the nineteenth century until almost the end of the century itself – local people began to look around for a means of, at least, ensuring that their newly straightened circumstances did not leave them completely at the horizontal.

As fashion deserted the inland resorts, on the one hand for Brighton and other coastal centres, on the other for the rigours of the new hydropathic cure centres, an immediate alternative future was to be found in developing the towns as residential centres, mainly for the retired and wealthy. At Bath this was not, at first, to entail much extra building, merely a general change in the occupants of already existing buildings. But, in most of the Regency spas – here including Tunbridge – as spa development froze newer residential building began to take place. It was mostly to be of the terrace and villa variety, though – as if these spas could not really believe that the great days of the immediate past were indeed at an end – the earlier tradition of building large houses and hotels for the more wealthy visitors did continue for some time.

In general it was from these later buildings that came the first indications that many of the spa towns really were in serious decline. As the nineteenth century advanced the wealthy no longer came to many of the older resorts – or, at least, not in such great numbers – preferring the rising resorts of Llandrindrod, Harrogate and Buxton and, later in the century, the fashionable watering-places of the Continent. Hotels and large houses came on to the market with increasing frequency, some to become hydros where the newer treatments were available, others offices and commercial premises, others to become schools. In almost all spas this latter development began in a small way – and for some remained just that. But, by the close of the century, the conversion of spa and other buildings for educational use had, in many places, drastically altered the function of the spa town. By then most had, to a greater or lesser degree, become school towns.

Many were ideally placed to exercise their new function. There existed commodious buildings which, at least to begin with, needed only the minimum of conversion. The spas already enjoyed a reputation as health centres – many emphasized their bracing air, their advantages of being removed from the smoke-ridden atmospheres of the industrial regions. They continued to enjoy the reputation of being acceptable social centres for the rising middle-class, both because it was largely this class that still visited the spas and because it was equally this class that now chose to settle in the newly created residential areas that surrounded the old spa centres. The spa towns enjoyed a middle class ambience as did few towns in England and, if the middle class had to send their children away to school, there could have been few places which would have been more in tune with their aspirations.

The new school promoters had, from an economic standpoint, two things running in their favour from the beginning. The first was the ready availability of relatively suitable buildings at comparatively low cost, the second was an equal availability of day-pupils from amongst the children of that considerable body of middle-class settlers who had already made the spas their home. Added to this were the possibilities of seemingly endless expansion, both in the acquisition of further premises – few other people were on the look-out for hotels in the declining spas – and in pupils, not only from the spas themselves, but from the rising middle class at large, especially those living in the suburban enclaves of the new industrial centres.

The spa schools had two other things working in their favour – unlikely companions, perhaps, but definitely linked – namely the pretentions of the new middle class itself and the

influence of Evangelicanism which had now spilled over from
the Methodist and other Free Churches and was running
rampant within the Church of England.

The middle class were not only largely cut off from the
educational preserves of the established upper class – the
aristocratic public schools such as Winchester and Eton
College – but were also increasingly opposed to them on a
number of grounds. The older schools had acquired, over the
previous century, an unfortunate reputation for vice and
indiscipline that thoroughly frightened Victorian *nouveau riche*
parents who, whilst wishing to see their children gain an entry
to the upper ranks of society via an education at such schools,
had never attended them themselves. This apart, many local
grammar schools, which had either not attempted or had
failed to make the transition to public school and which would
normally have been considered quite adequate to give a good
middle-class education, were in decline for a number of
reasons. These included disinterest on the part of local
administraters, misappropriation of funds, inflexible
interpretations of the terms of original charters and charitable
bequests and, most of all, the fact that they, like the majority
of the public schools offered, not a commercial, liberal,
middle-class education but one firmly based upon the
Classics. This bias the new bourgeoisie saw as increasingly
irrelevant to their own place in a society now dominated by
commerce and industrial development rather than by the
traditional aristocratic basis of power, the land, the Church
and military and govermental service. In short, the new
middle class desired an education that would prepare the
future professional man and the future businessman. Existing
education was found wanting, from their point of view, largely
because it catered for what they considered an irrelevance in
the progressive society of the nineteenth century, i.e., the
gentleman, whose educational lineage went back more than
three centuries to the founding of most of the grammar schools
of Tudor times.

Reforms in both directions, in morality and in restructuring
of the syllabus, did move ahead in some of the better known
schools, such as the Rugby of Thomas Arnold and the

Shrewsbury of Samuel Butler. But reform was a slow business and, anyway, it was no easier to get a boy into a 'good school' then than nowadays. From the point of view of established school bodies it was a 'seller's market' and there were just not enough places at the older schools to take all the new middle-class pupils who could be found to fill them. In a free-flowing economic situation the solution was found by pricing most of the new middle class out of the market. Faced by this, and a host of connected problems, the creation of new schools to cater almost exclusively for the needs of the Victorian middle class was an inevitability. They were by no means to be located exclusively at the former spa centres. But the existence of so many factors favourable to the creation of schools at these centres made it almost equally inevitable that the more enterprising of the old spas should share very prominently in the new school boom.

Another, and very important, factor leading to the establishment of new and essentially middle-class schools at this time was the glaring absence of any provision for the formal education of girls. There were, of course, governesses who carried out most of the duties of the private tutor and, along slightly more formal lines, the finishing schools which had, for example, blossomed in such profusion at eighteenth-century Bath. But the finishing schools were scarcely in existence to provide a 'young lady' with an education, rather, as in the case of Thackeray's Becky Sharpe, to provide her with the social ammunition whereby to achieve a 'good match'. Good governesses were, on the other hand, hard to come by – though mediocre examples of the breed were plentiful enough. This was mainly because few governesses would be expected to be much better than their own restricted education had allowed. The new middle class had a ready realisation that women in their situation required an education which at least gave them a comprehension of the society in which they lived. The new middle-class woman was not to be a mere adornment and match-making schemer after the eighteenth-century model but, instead, at least the social and intellectual equal of her partner.

All these requirements of an emergent class were to be most

obviously met at the most rapidly declining of all the major spa towns – namely Cheltenham. Here the Evangelical influence was to steadily increase under the impact of Dean Francis Close who was, apart from his opposition to race-meetings, theatres and Cheltenham's Regency hang-over, also a keen advocate of education provided that it was imbued with Christian precepts, rather than 'the abominations' of Classical authors.

Close was not merely interested in middle-class education, but in Evangelical education over the whole social spectrum. In Cheltenham he was associated with the founding of a number of working-class schools which mainly concerned themselves with the 'three Rs' and religious principles according to the precepts of the Church of England Evangelical party. He was also responsible for the creation of two teacher training colleges, one for men, one for women, initially to staff the working-class schools in Cheltenham but later to be trained to inculcate Evangelical principles over a far wider area. But the foundations still to be most closely associated with his name are Cheltenham College, Cheltenham Ladies' College and Pate's Grammar School – the latter an institution which he succeeded in resuscitating after a long period of decline and neglect.

The foundation charter of Cheltenham College well revealed the pretensions of the town's new middle class, certainly in so far as the founding committee were concerned. Though they were, to a considerable extent, priced out of the older public schools and, from an economic point of view at least, were therefore found to be wanting as 'gentlemen' of the eighteenth-century mould, they nevertheless considered that they came well within their new interpretation of the term. The founding charter declared that "only gentlemen" were to be allowed to take out shares in the new undertaking, "no retail trader being under any circumstances considered". This meant that anyone above the condition of a retail trader was eligible to be considered a gentleman i.e., the professional and business classes. This would have been an interpretation that many of the older schools could scarcely have considered appropriate. Here a 'gentleman' was a term which could only with difficulty be stretched to include the clergyman and middle-ranking military officer.

Cheltenham College was to exhibit, in its early years, all those qualities which marked off the middle class proprietory schools from their older rivals. An Evangelical influence was to surplant that of the Classics, modern subjects figured in the curriculum and the College benefited considerably in this direction by the fact that both the Army and the Civil Service was now to be thrown open to public competition. The new middle class had long rankled at the 'purchase system' which had applied in these fields with the result that they had largely turned their backs on them as forms of employment. But, as soon as they were opened to competition, almost all the new middle class schools then in existence opened sides which actively prepared their pupils for the examinations. In later years certain schools were opened which had the passing of either the military services or the civil services examinations as almost their sole reasons for existence.

These new schools, of which those at the spa towns – such as the ones already mentioned at Cheltenham and others of which Malvern College, Harrogate Ladies College, Bath's Kingswood School and Lansdowne Proprietory School (now the Royal School) and Brighton College – form some of the most outstanding examples, were part of an educational revolution which continued without parallel until the end of the nineteenth century. By then state and civic initiative had produced compulsory elementary education, from 1902 was to sponsor the civic grammar schools and was already involved in the beginnings of the 'red-brick' university which was intended to supplement those of Oxford and Cambridge. It may be a matter of passing interest to observe that no spa town – with the exception of Brighton, which enjoyed a somewhat different development – was destined to become a new university town at that time.

But, alongside the development of the new proprietory colleges, came the complementary development of their 'feeder' institutions, the preparatory schools. This secondary development lagged a little behind that of the proprietory colleges themselves but, by the last quarter of the nineteenth century, it was well under way. It was here that the former spa centres were to make a real mark with preparatory schools blossoming in almost all of them. A number were short-lived and many were not to survive the doldrums of the 1930s. Some, however, such as Malvern's Link School, are still in existence and, whilst many of the older preparatory schools have died, others have been born in their place. With today's frightened flight from the rumoured terrors of 'new' State primary teaching methods and the general implementation of the comprehensive system the stage is more than set for a further expansion of the spa-town preparatory schools.

Cheltenham's Proprietory College – later Cheltenham College – was to be the first public school to be founded in the reign of Queen Victoria. Its President was Lord Sherborne while Francis Close and the Rev J. Browne of Holy Trinity were Vice Presidents. The committee consisted of thirty-six shareholders and faithfully reflected the new Cheltenham establishment of Evangelical Toryism of which Francis Close was the epitome – Colonel Berkeley is noticeable by his absence from this committee.

The school was opened in 1841 in temporary accommodation in Bayshill Terrace, which was considered a very good site as it was near the centre of the town. This consideration was unusual for a public school, which was normally to value relative isolation from large settlements. In Cheltenham's case, however, it was a sensible one, especially in the College's early years, for it was to draw a very high proportion of its pupils from the town itself on a day-boy basis. In 1843 the nucleus of the present school was opened, the Tudor Gothic schoolrooms of 'Big Classical' and 'Big Modern' sited on either side of a central tower – though 'Big Modern' was not finally completed until 1850. Delays in building may have been connected to a crisis of confidence in the new school engendered by rioting and bullying that, initially, brought it well into line with its older rivals. This was to be partially solved by the sacking of its first Principal, the Rev Dr Albert Philips, an intransigent Evangelical, and his replacement by William Dobson who, unusually for Headmasters of the time, actually liked boys and considered they were good for other things than an education calculated to make them into minor prophets.

Although Cheltenham College for many years drew the majority of its pupils from the town and nearby countryside this picture was slowly to alter. At its opening less than half the pupils had been boarders but, within thirty years, this had been completely reversed and the College was taking boys from all over the country. It was not, and never could have been the case with the next Cheltenham educational institution in which Francis Close was to take a hand.

Pate's Grammar School was an Elizabethan foundation, endowed by Richard Pate, a local boy made good, being successively a scholar of Corpus Christi, Oxford, a student of Lincoln's Inn, Member of Parliament for Gloucester and Recorder for that city. Elizabeth made over to him the lands of Cheltenham's disestablished chantry – part of which was already being used to maintain a school – and Richard Pate in his turn made over the lands to Corpus Christi on the condition that three-quarters of the revenue should to to the maintainance of a school in Cheltenham and a separate almshouse. The schoolmaster received £16 a year from the profits of a field adjoining the schoolhouse. It was a grammar school of the general Tudor type with Latin and Greek being taught, but with more emphasis on English and mathematics than was usual at the time. The schoolbuilding, which could accommodate up to fifty pupils, stood on the north side of the High Street, its site now occupied by modern supermarkets.

By the time that Francis Close and "the Vestry Committee of resolute men" took an interest in the old school it was in a very bad way indeed. Up until 1815 the master had been paid no more than the £16 laid down in Elizabethan times, although the value of the endowments had greatly increased since then. Pupils were paying for subjects other than Latin and Greek and the new salary offered to the master, £30, was not enough to attract men of sufficient ability. The building itself was in decay and the number of pupils had fallen to thirty-four – an abysmally low figure considering that Victorian Cheltenham's population was many times larger than that of the Elizabethan town.

Pressure was put on the Fellows of Corpus Christi, who were accused of mismanagement and of misappropriation of Trust funds. Eventually Corpus Christi yielded and in 1848 the old building was closed. In 1852 it reopened with a new headmaster, a revised scheme of instruction and a new classroom. Four years later the school had 150 pupils, a waiting list as long again and no fears for its future. In more modern times the Victorian school-buildings – erected in 1887 to replace Cheltenham's last Tudor survival – have disappeared and the school has moved – as Cheltenham Grammar School – to a new site in the western suburbs. Pate's name had, however, been preserved in the title of the Grammar School's sister foundation as Pate's Grammar School for Girls. It is a rather curious state of affairs as Richard Pate made no provisions for female education – Tudor England, despite Queen Bess, was not exactly to be found echoing with the war-cries of Womens' Lib – and the poor man's ghost would probably find it all too much, if he re-visited Cheltenham, to discover piped music and pre-packed 'food' on the site of his original school and delightful young women apparently masquerading as boys at the school which enjoys his name.

Francis Close was also to be associated with the founding of a "proprietory College for the education of young ladies" – later to be more simply known as Cheltenham Ladies' College. Close was elected president of the school which opened in 1853 at Cambray House, where Wellington had stayed when visiting the spa in 1816, and which was now dedicated to providing a "first rate education to the Daughters and young children of Noblemen and Gentlemen". The daughters of retail traders could hardly have expected to get a mention. The school adopted a more liberal curriculum than that at the boys' College and included Grammar, Georgraphy, History, Arithmetic, French and Music – to these were added Needlework and Drawing and study of the "Holy Scripture and the Liturgy of the Church of England". While Close was not entirely absent from the affairs of the new school he was to take much less interest in it than in the boys' establishment, probably because he was not entirely convinced of the need for such an ambitious project which may have seemed to go further than his own ideas in regard to women's education.

The school was to run through much the same problems as those first experienced at the boys' college. At first there were two co-Principals in the form of Mrs Proctor, widow of a local colonel, and her daughter Anne. These soon developed strained relations with the School Council and, as a result of indiscipline and near-rioting which proved that Cheltenham's young ladies could be decidedly unladylike if they chose, the school's numbers steadily declined. In 1858 the Proctors were dismissed to be replaced by Miss Dorothea Beale, a dynamic personality who was to reign as Principal for forty-eight years, dying, still in harness, in 1906 at the age of seventy-five. It was Dorothea Beale who was responsible for the almost continuous expansion of the College during her lifetime, both in new buildings and in pupils. By the time of her death the College, which had long ago moved from its original premises, was renowned as the foremost girls' school in the world.

Cheltenham's three Close-influenced schools were soon to be joined by another, posthumous addition. Close left Cheltenham to become Dean of Carlisle in 1856 – but his influence lingered. When, in 1882, he died, the townspeople were at pains to provide a fitting memorial to their clerical regenerator. After various proposals had been put forward – if Colonel Berkeley had still been alive one would possibly have been a gallows – it was finally decided to commemorate him by the establishment of a school on the lines he had so fervently advocated himself. Thus was born, in 1886, the Dean Close Memorial School with its first Headmaster in Dr W.H. Flecker, lately of the City of London Collegiate School. He was a strong Evangelical, but was also an adroit manager and, during the years of his headmastership, built up the school's numbers from a mere forty at its foundation to over two hundred. The school fixed its sights a little lower than Cheltenham College, aiming to give a public school education at the minimum of cost and with the emphasis on spiritual values. Rather naturally, in its early years, it seems to have attracted the offspring of a considerable number of clergymen.

Its first headmaster was the father of the poet and dramatist James Elroy Flecker. His verse drama *Hassan* created a considerable stir when it was first staged. The poet died in Switzerland in 1914 where he had gone in an effort to combat the consumption from which he suffered for so long. Today Dean Close School has expanded and new boarding houses have been added along the Lansdown Road.

Another Midland spa which was to become even more of a school-town than Cheltenham – though was not to emulate it with three public schools to its name – was Malvern. By 1890 there were twenty-five private schools of various types in the town and Malvern College had been established in 1863. Important as Malvern College was to become it was the smaller schools which were to be more of an influence here – the preparatory and private schools, with their attendant staff and pupils, were to provide it with a bias as marked as when it was the domain of the hydropaths.

It was, of course, the hydropaths who had been responsible for Malvern becoming a school town in the first place. As hydropathy and the 'water cure' in general went into a deepening dive in the mid-nineteenth century the hydros themselves came on the market and, in many cases, were bought up by people who had not the slightest intention of keeping them going as money-losing cure establishments. The town was ideally situated to promote its new function. It was elevated, breezy, bracing and already had a reputation for health – something highly valued by Victorian middle-class parents. Surprisingly, to modern ears, it also emphasized that it was especially well drained. Premises were relatively easy to come by and religious principles were espoused by the majority of their new proprietors – no one in Malvern was going to be called 'experimental' or 'progressive'. Added to this was, on the part of many of the new institutions, a calculated brand of snobbishness that appealed to the new bourgeoisie and, in the nearby Midland industrial towns, quite enough of that new bourgeoisie to keep at least the best of the schools in business.

Hillside, at West Malvern, founded by the Rev Edward Ford, was one of the better-equipped of the boys' preparatory schools, boasting a swimming bath, chapel and gymnasium. May Place at Malvern Wells and Southlea at Great Malvern also enjoyed considerable reputations and, in comparison to many of their rivals, were long-lived. In 1899 The Priory School was opened, surviving until 1929, when it was bought by the urban district council who converted it into their offices, also enlarging the former school swimming-baths and opening them to the public. Still in existence is the Link School, founded in Great Malvern in 1860. Later it was moved and took over its present building in 1885 following the closure of the railway hotel.

These schools, and others like them, were an important element in preventing Malvern from becoming just one more declining spa and were important in themselves. They also helped to establish a tradition that is still maintained, in that the majority of preparatory schools are to be found in towns whilst the majority of public schools are, or originally were, sited in comparative isolation – even what is, perhaps, the foremost of modern preparatory schools, the blue corduroy-clad Dragon School, not moving from urban Oxford. They belonged to a period when the preparatory school was regarded as almost as important as the public school and when it developed a mystique and mythology all its own. Perhaps this was because a very large number of preparatory school pupils did not go on to public school and formed, in a later social strata, a type of lesser gentleman who occupied the intermediate rungs of the ladder a little below the public school type yet well above the remainder of the social mixture.

The Bishop of Worcester was the first President of the Malvern Proprietory College Company, with Dr Leopold Sturmmes – who had given most of the land – as Secretary and Fredrick Lygon (later Sixth Earl Beauchamp) as Chairman. At the outset Malvern took the older public schools as its inspiration, declaring in its prospectus that it "Had been established ... on the model of the great public schools, for educating the Sons of Gentlemen at moderate cost."

Its first Headmaster was the Rev A. Faber and the school is said to have been modelled on a design originally intended for Clifton College, prepared by Charles Hanson. The school was designed to accommodate six hundred boys and this target had been reached by the turn of the century. New building also took place, including laboratories, a sanatorium, a gymnasium and a chapel designed by Sir Arthur Bloomfield which was completed in 1899.

Like Cheltenham, however, Malvern had also moved ahead in the provision of private education for girls. The Girls' College grew from a kindergarten established in 1893 until, by 1919, it had established itself securely enough to be able to purchase the Imperial Hotel. The school was further enlarged in 1934 by the addition of York Hall. Many of the earlier girls' schools failed to survive, including Wellington House, whose headmistress seems to have been appropriately nicknamed 'The General' both by her pupils and by the local people. She was accustomed to escort her pupils on their Sunday hill-walking excursions mounted on a spirited cob. Malvern Wells boasted two girls' schools, The Manse and Cambridge House, while at Malvern Link were The Birches and Hazel Bank. Some schools were very small and had to struggle for their existence in what became a very competitive market. Others succeeded well enough and were not to founder until hit by the impact of the Great War and the straightened circumstances of the 1930s. Some of the latter schools were, in many ways, re-groupings of older ones and, in this guise, have survived into our own times.

Undoubtedly many were unremarkable and some were downright opportunist ventures. But many brought advantages to the area and certainly were largely responsible in seeing that Malvern did not lapse into a state of stagnation after the collapse of its 'water cure' industry. Many of the teachers took an active part in the social affairs of the town and, without them it is possible that Malvern would never have had a sufficient body of interest for it to have been able to make the next step in its development – which was to lead to it becoming a festival centre.

Many of the smaller spas did not succeed in making this mid-century transition into the school town. Spas such as Shropshire's Church Stretton, Wiltshire's Holt and Worcestershire's Tenbury Wells never really developed on a sufficient scale for there to be either enough large buildings or a sufficient resident middle class population for the general school-town phase ever to take off.

Some smaller spas did, however, deny this trend, such as Clifton which, with its hot wells, had functioned as an over-flow spa to Bath from the eighteenth to the mid-nineteenth century. But Clifton, by the time its College was built in 1861, had developed largely as a middle-class suburb of nearby Bristol and its development had long ceased to be along traditional spa-town lines.

On the other hand, two of the larger spa towns, Leamington and Droitwich, although they were to develop as school-towns of the small, private school type, were not to acquire prestigious undertakings on the lines of Malvern College or Cheltenham Ladies' College. In the case of Droitwich the reason for this may be found in the fact that the town, at the time of the nineteenth-century school-boom, could not have been termed an ailing spa. It was a later development than the older spas and based its treatments upon different methods than those practised by the Malvern hydropaths. Its hotels were full and the middle-class had not yet begun to forsake their large houses. This apart it was essentially a visitors' town, middle-class settlement not being intense, and there still remained a substantial industrial quarter – the salt industry – All of these were factors which meant that it could not hope, and did not aspire, to enter the school-town league. To a lesser extent the same was true of Leamington, whose spa facilities came to be continued under what amounted to municipal enterprise. It was also early to adopt the status of an inland resort essentially divorced from its old spa activities, to launch itself as a tourist centre as 'The Gateway to the Shakespeare Country' – an effort which succeeded in keeping its hotels full. Schools did, of course, blossom here, but not in such an overwhelming profusion as to give the town a marked bias in this direction.

To some extent this was also to be true of Bath where, although many schools were to be founded during the nineteenth century, the town was already sufficiently diversified to be largely capable of absorbing the new development without the danger of being submerged by it. Both of Bath's larger schools of the post-spa period, Kingswood School and the Lansdown Proprietory College (later to be known as the Royal School, Bath) were to be originally designed by James Wilson, who had already designed the central block at Cheltenham College. Prior Park, the former home of Ralph Allen, had already been converted into a Catholic College and Lansdown Proprietory College was to change its function before it finally settled down to welcome the Royal School.

Lansdown began life in 1852 as Lansdown Proprietory College for Boys – but, twelve years later, it was to be closed, then re-opened as the Royal School "for the daughters of Army officers". It, therefore never had the widespread net that was available to Cheltenham Ladies' College. Its aims were correspondingly more limited and the Royal School settled down to a relatively quiet existence, apparently quite satisfied not to occupy a front-seat in the annals of women's education.

Kingswood School was an educational immigrant, having been first established at Bristol in 1748. It was founded by John Wesley – who enjoyed a little notoriety in the religious contentions of the day – for the sons of the more thrifty Methodists who regarded the regimes of the existing public schools as being too far out of line with the principles of their religious faith. It was, however, from its inception, devoted to what was, for the time, an extremely wide curriculum. In 1768 Wesley outlined the purposes of Kingswood School:

> Our design is, with God's assistance, to train up children in every branch of useful learning. We teach none but boarders. These are taken in, being between the years of six and twelve, in order to be taught reading, writing, arithmetic, English, French, Latin, Greek, Hebrew, history, geography, chronology, rhetoric, logic, ethics, geometry, algebra, physics and music.

Despite this very liberal curriculum, however, the school was conducted on the strictest lines and must have been something of a combination of a monastery and an instructional factory. Boys rose, all the year round, at 4.00 a.m. to spend an hour in prayer and religious reading. This was followed by a communal hour and another hour of work before the 7.00 a.m. breakfast. School work then took up the morning until 11.00 a.m. with a two hour break for dinner before school-work was resumed for the four hours up to 5.00 p.m. Supper was followed by a public service at 7.00 p.m. and bed at 8.00 p.m. Wesley was to state that "neither do we allow any time for play on any day". It was a six-day week and games were forbidden in favour of gardening.

This discipline was to prove too great for many boys and, after 1796, only the sons of Methodist ministers were admitted. It was in this form that the school transferred to Bath in 1852.

Away to the north, Harrogate became associated with the school-town boom somewhat late in the day, if only because it was itself essentially a latter-day spa. As has already been observed, although Harrogate was in existence as a spa from the end of the sixteenth century, it was not until the early decades of the nineteenth century that it had sufficiently developed to be able to free itself from the apron-strings of nearby Knaresborough. Knaresborough had an endowed grammar school – the King James's Grammar School – which seems to have been founded along conventional grammar school lines. It seems to have experienced difficult times and emerged into the nineteenth century in a most confused state – something which was hardly helped when its master, the Rev James Noake, absconded with the school records in 1809. There were also private schools of various complexion and Richardson's Charity School, which had been founded in 1765. One Knaresborough private school teacher, Eugene Aram, was to create a considerable furore when he was hanged in 1759 for the murder of one Daniel Clarke.

Slowly developing Harrogate naturally lagged behind its more established neighbour in the provision of educational facilities. In 1833 Harrogate possessed two boarding schools, one of which went by the title of Catherine Parry's Ladies' Seminary, as well as the Free School of Bilton-with-Harrogate, an endowed school for local children founded by Richard Taylor in 1779. Harrogate was not really to begin to develop as anything approaching a school-town until the 1880s, by which time the Victorian revitalisation of the spa was well under way, with a considerable body of middle-class residents already permanently settled in the town. This school-town development was in no way to replace the spa development as had been the case in Malvern and Cheltenham. Harrogate, as a spa, was at this time very far from dead – and indeed looked forward to even greatest expansion as England's premier spa of the Edwardian period. Harrogate was, therefore, to be both a spa town and a school-town – with the school aspect to be no more than secondary to its main development.

In 1868 Bilton Grange School was founded as a boarding school for children of "the upper classes". Like those that were destined to follow it Bilton Grange made as much capital as it could out of Harrogate's healthy situation and the reputation it was acquiring, like other spas before it, of possessing a dominantly middle-class presence. Western College was founded in 1873 as a "select Private Boarding and Day School for the sons of Merchants, Professional men, etc", and between 1870 and 1895 a rash of similiarly intentioned private schools were opened, including Trinity College, Westminster School, Ellesmere College and Harrogate College.

Of these new foundations Harrogate College was probably to prove the most important and influential, especially under its first headmaster, G.M. Savery. Savery was for some time the educational colossus of Harrogate, elevating his own school to the point where it acquired a very considerable and distinguished reputation. He was also to be, in 1893, the moving spirit behind the foundation of the Harrogate Ladies' College and was a determined advocate of women's education. He was largely instrumental in bringing to Harrogate the university extension courses organised by Oxford and Cambridge – something which helped to give it the reputation of being rather more than a well-patronised social centre.

Buxton, too, has its clustering of private schools though, like Leamington, nothing in the big-name category, and even Lincolnshire's early twentieth-century spa, Woodall, can claim to possess its preparatory school for boys. In fact, most of the spas have their school cluster though, as already said, some of the smaller spas never reached this stage and it is a development notably absent from members of the Welsh order.

Brighton, though leaving the spa league at a rather early date, was nevertheless to produce Brighton College and, in more recent times, to become the seat of the new University of Sussex. (Of all the 'concrete universities' of the late 1950s and early 60s this was the one which was heralded as the twentieth-century challenge to Oxbridge – distinguished staff, promising students. Unfortunately the promise appears to have largely evaporated, and the university seems to have settled back to a level with its contemporaries at Norwich, Lancaster, Bradford and elsewhere.)

The founding principles behind Brighton College had much in common with those of Malvern and Cheltenham. The school was founded in 1847 at Portland House, Portland Place and did not move to its present site in Eastern Road until 1849. The College was launched by a group of prominent local residents to provide "a thoroughly liberal and practical education in conformity with the principles of the Established Church". It was a line which might well have been written by Francis Close himself. It took more than another thirty years before all the main school buildings were complete, though of these all but the main schoolroom was to be designed by Gilbert Scott – taking time off from 'restoring' the nation's churches. The College's original buildings were to become a part of the St Dunstan's Institute for the Blind.

Tunbridge Wells was also to sprout its private schools, headed by Tunbridge School though, as in the case of Malvern, the development was to be more marked in the number of preparatory schools. These still exist in considerable numbers though, for its size, Tunbridge cannot be said to compare with Malvern in this respect, although it is possibly its closest rival. Langton Green and Rosehill both have long histories and good reputations but Tunbridge has one rather more unusual establishment in the field. This is the Waguelin School of Russian Ballet, which takes boys and girls from the ages of six to seventeen and, which faced by an upsurge of interest in its main subject, shows no signs of flagging.

In the 1930s many of the smaller spa schools went out of business and the requisitioning of school premises in the early years of the Second World War almost forced some of the larger schools to follow them. Nowadays there are fewer school-party crocodiles moving across the slopes of Malvern's hills and the parks of Cheltenham and Harrogate. But many schools still remain and, if anything, are more fitfully in business today than they have been at any time since the turn of the century. It may, perhaps, be a state of affairs which cannot long be expected to continue in the time of a newer, and more far-reaching educational revolution than that presaged by the foundation of the nineteenth-century, proprietory colleges and their smaller brethren. But one thing is unalterable fact. The schools have, in many spas, been as much a part of their history as the waters which once made them.

11

And So To?

At the beginning of the twentieth century's final quarter the immediate future development of most of the former major spa towns seems to be progressing along lines already established. As we have already seen the life-blood of the remaining spas was almost drained dry in the relatively austere years between the two World Wars, and the Second World War provided the ultimate death knell for the old kind of spa life as it had survived in such redoubts as Harrogate.

Present day spa centres seem to have opted for the role of festival towns or conference centres, as in the case of Harrogate and Cheltenham, for that of leisure centres-cum-touring resorts as at Llandrindrod Wells, or for a mixture of both with increasing residential development and some small, low profile industrialism as in Droitwich or Leamington. The latter developments have meant that many spas are no longer the middle-class biased towns they once were, though in most cases that bias still remains. In this respect perhaps Cheltenham and Leamington have changed most radically, Cheltenham especially having sprouted large new housing areas in recent years which have so altered its complexion that it no longer warrants its traditional associations with gouty colonels and old ladies in bath chairs.

Bath chairs, of course, still survive in some of the spas, most notably at Leamington which still dispenses hydropathic treatments under the National Health service and on the most up to date lines. In other spas 'the cure' may be available privately as at Llandrindrod or Buxton. But 'the cure' is now most certainly a fringe occupation at the modern English spa town. Llandrindrod and Buxton have bid for a popular image as tourist and recreation centres, Llandrindrod in relation to mid Wales and Buxton in relation to the High Peak. Buxton, like other spas, has its shopping fortnight, but it also attempts to be the English equivalent of Scotland's Aviemore, in the winter months concentrating on skiing, tobogganing and curling. Leamington is cast in something of the same pattern claiming to be the centre for the Shakespeare Country and making much of its shopping facilities. It is also an 'events' town and still keeps up its tradition of mounting sporting attractions.

Harrogate and Bath each have their festivals – that at Harrogate having formed a connection with the works of the Russian composer Shostakovitch. Bath has two festivals, the Bath Festival and the annual Bach Festival, the later founded as long ago as 1946. The Bath Festival is closely associated with Yehudi Menuhin and his sister Hepzibah and in recent years, Sir Michael Tippet has played an increasingly important role.

Cheltenham has its Literary Festival – though some of its glory seems to have departed for the nearby festival at Stroud – and even Brighton has joined the ranks of the culturally conscious. Brighton's strength, however, would seem to lie in its French and Italian weeks and as a resort which has begun to draw not only the English visitor but his Continental counterpart as well. Even the small spa of Church Stretton is in the festival ranks and the Malvern Festival, with its memories of Elgar and Bernard Shaw, still survives fitfully into our own day.

The spa towns were amongst the first to mount these annual gatherings of organised edification. But now, so it would seem, almost everywhere has its festival and the position of the spas in this respect is far from being unchallenged. With their ample facilities it may be that those who are able will ultimately develop increasingly along the more popular lines of Buxton and Llandrindrod.

Despite changing conditions the middle class ambience of the spa towns still remains. Some like Tunbridge and Harrogate are near enough to large business centres to have developed a considerable commuter population. In others the retired element amongst the population is still large and not all the new houses going up around Cheltenham could be claimed to be intended for the late twentieth-century equivalent of the Victorian's industrious artisan.

Private education still prospers in such towns as Cheltenham, Harrogate and Malvern. The preparatory system has been rather sensitive to economic conditions and, even now, could not claim to be as strong as it was in the 1920s. But, in this area of education, this is a period of growth as middle class parents increasingly opt for preparatory education as the essential insurance required to keep their children outside the State comprehensive system. In an uncertain political climate just how long this situation will persist it would be impossible to forecast.

The proprietory colleges of such spas as Malvern and Cheltenham appear relatively unassailable. Like the preparatory schools they, are at the moment, in a state of boom. Yet it would be a brave body of men who would now subscribe the funds to found a new one.

Some spas appear about to be stripped of all but the vestiges of their health and leisure past. Droitwich is perhaps, the most threatened with plans for increasing development on its outskirts and with only niggardly attempts being made to re-invigorate its civic amenities. It is the spa with the greatest prospect of being submerged, for planned development here is on such a scale as will probably obliterate the traditional character of Corbett's town.

Tunbridge Wells is already submerged – but in a different way. The town is now one of the most favoured of London's commuter settlements and, behind its spa town facades, is really as suburbanised as Kingston or Cheam. It preserves its Pantiles rather like a child will treasure its first cast-off milk-tooth. Here there is held its open air 'Shakespeare Week'. But, in general, it would appear to want to have little to do with festivals or Tibetan Weeks. It is quite well off without them, thank you.

Brighton and Scarborough – and the other towns which once saw life as coastal spas – no longer have a spa identity at all, though Scarborough still appears to bear some antipathy to its inland rival, Harrogate. But the coastal spas are now seaside resorts and once again are locked in battle with the inland spas. Nowadays battle is most closely joined on the conference-centre front, for with Continental package holidays making inroads into the traditional seaside clientèle, the coastal towns have seen their future lying in the development of their facilities for the gatherings of every group from science fiction enthusiasts to the annual breast-beatings of our political parties. The gatherings of these two species are, in many ways, not markedly dissimilar.

If other spas follow the example of Buxton and Llandrindrod the coastal resorts will be placed even more upon their mettle. Llandrindrod already has its Pleasurama which caters for everything from bingo to trampolining. For those who like the memory of the spa it also has, amongst other things, the Metropole Hotel. But its attractions, in the main, lie outside the resort itself and it has a hinterland which few coastal resorts can offer. Here there is unspoilt scenery, good fishing, uncluttered space for almost inevitably repressed, urbanised children and the general feeling of being 'away from it all' is easily obtained in an environment happily free from the worst expressions of the gregarious, holidaying English. With rivers free from industrial effluent, a general absence of industry itself and an agriculture which makes only minor demands on the products of the fertiliser and pesticide revolution, this area of mid Wales can justly claim to be one of the least polluted in Britain. The same can hardly be said for the spalet of Church Stretton whose Cardingmill Valley has mushroomed an Alpine cafeteria, hot-dog and ice-cream vans and a trail of litter that stretches to the top of the Long Mynd itself.

So where do we go from here? Civic societies, and their equivalents, will no doubt continue to act as watchdogs to help insure that at least the image on the English spa town will remain intact – though, in the case of Bath, their efforts have so far been hopeful rather than successful. But the image is by implication hardly the reality. This latter would seem to be that the spas will continue to function as leisure centres in all but those centres where such a development has now been rendered impossible by projected planning considerations or where they have already turned their back upon their past. In fact, these garden towns are in many ways ready-built leisure parks. In them leisure and recreation has already begun to return to an urbanised setting. Like it or not our country is destined to become increasingly urbanised. Perhaps in the increasing development of the former spas as leisure centres we have already witnessed the beginning of the end of the near-panic of the nineteenth- and twentieth-century flight from the towns. For urban England it may be our only salvation. The spas have proved that urbanisation need not be a concrete jungle. In this age they have much to teach us – especially when we realise that our already dwindling open countryside cannot last forever.

SELECT BIBLIOGRAPHY

Addison, William, *English Spas*, Batsford, 1951.

Atkinson, T.R., *Local Style in English Architecture*, Batsford, 1947

Clarke, Frank L., *New Light on Epsom Wells*, Pullinger's, Epsom, 1953

Cunliffe, Barry, *Roman Bath*, Routledge & Kegan Paul, 1971

Dale, Anthony, *History and Architecture of Brighton*, S.R. Publishers Ltd., 1972

Edwards, K.C. *The Peak District*, Collins, 1962

Forester, H. *The Smaller Queen Anne and Georgian House*. Friends of Historic Essex. Essex County Record Office 1964

Freeman, Rodgers and Kinvig. *Lancashire, Cheshire and the Isle of Man*. Nelson. 1966

Gardener, Brian. *The Public Schools*. Hamish Hamilton, 1973

Granville, A.B., *The Spas of England*. Vols 1 & 2. pub. 1841. reprinted 1971

Harris, Bohn. *Georgian Country Houses*. Country Life Books, 1868.

Harrison, J.F.C., *The Early Victorians*. Weidenfeld & Nicholson

Hearsey, John. *The Young Mr Pepys*. Constable, 1973

Halevy, Elie. *Victorian Years*. Benn, reprinted 1961

Hern, Anthony. *The Seaside Holiday*. Cresset, 1967

Jennings, Bernard. *A History of the Wells and Spas of Harrogate*. Harrogate Corporation, 1974

Lees-Milne, James. *The Age of Adam*, Batsford, 1947

Lehmann, E.L., *Epsom Spa*, Surrey Archaeological Society Transations, 1974

Little, Bryan, *The Building of Bath*, Collins, 1947

McGrath, Patrick (ed) *Bristol in the Eighteenth Century*, David & Charles, 1972

Margetson, Stella, *Leisure & Pleasure in the Eighteenth Century*, Cassell, 1970

Musgrave, Clifford, *Life in Brighton*, Faber, 1970

Pakenhem, Simona, *Cheltenham*, Macmillan, 1971

Pearsall, Ronald, *Edwardian Life & Leisure*, David & Charles, 1973

Priestley, J.B., *The Prince Regent*, Heinemann
Ramsey, S.C., *Smaller Georgian Houses and their Details, 1750-1820*, Architectural Press, 1972
Rowntree, A, *A History of Scarborough*, 1931
Smith, Brian S., *History of Malvern*, Leicester University Press, 1964
Smith, Anthony, *Beside the Seaside*, Allen & Unwin, 1972
Smith, R.A.L., *Bath*, Batsford, 1944
Sitwell, Osbert/Bartom, Margaret, *Brighton*, Faber, 1948.
Steers, J.A., *The Coastline of England & Wales*, Cambridge University Press, 1969
A History of the Royal Pavilion Brighton, Country Life Books, 1939
Turner, E.S., *Taking the Cure*, Michael Joseph
Waite, Vincent, *The Bristol Hot Well*, Bristol University Branch of the Historical Association, 1964
Wood, G. Bernard, *Yorkshire*, Batsford, 1967

INDEX

Abbott, William, 40
Alford, 31
Alfred the Great, King, 16
Allen, Ralph, 30, 79-82, 153, 175
Alvanley, Willian Second Baron, 92
Allworthy, Squire, 181
Anne, Queen, 24, 29, 149
Anne of Nodena, 27
Arkwright, Richard, 69
Arnold, Thomas, 163
Arthritis, 71, 133
Astrop, 20
Austen, Jane, 11, 156
Aviemore, 181

Bach Festival, 181
Baldwin, Thomas, 114, 115
Barbary Corsairs, 85
Barge, Martin, 163
Barnet, 21
Bath, 11, 25, 27-31, 34, 56, 73, 76-84, 103, 113, 119-124, 145-153, 174-176, 183
Bath Festival, 181
Bath Olivers, 76
Baths: Attendants, 142, 146, 148
   Brine, 63, 133
   Medieval, 15, 75, 148
   Music at, 77
   Public, 77
   Roman, 145-146
Beale, Dorothea, 170
Beckington, Thomas, 15
Ben Rhydding, 96

Berkley Castle (Glos.), 37
Berkeley, Narbone, Lord Botetort, 85
Berkeley, William Fitzhardinge, 37-38, 45-46, 153
Bernhardt, Sarah, 52
Bilton Grange School, 177
Bladud, King, 13
Blackpool, 103, 117
Blomfield, Sir Arthur, 172
Borrow, George, 68
Bournemouth, 105
Bowling Greens, 149
Braganza, Catherine of, 23, 28, 149
Breeze, Christopher, 127
Bright, Dr Timothy, 21
Brighton, 27, 30, 34, 90-93, 103, 105, 106-112, 127-128, 158
Brighton Camp, 109-110
Brighton College, 178-179
Brighton Pavilion, 129-130
Brighton Races, 111-112
Browne, Rev. J., 167
Browne, Lancelot, 31, 83
Brummel, George, 72, 90-93
Bucketting, 125
Builth Wells, 65-66
Burke, Edmund, 109
Burton, Decimus, 23, 124-125, 126-128, 129, 130, 133
Busby, Charles, 127-128, 129
Butler, Samuel, 164
Buxton, 13, 32, 53, 66-69, 114, 117-118, 126, 143, 161, 180-181

Calais, 65, 92
Card, Rev. Henry, 59
Cardingmill Valley (Salop) 64
Carlisle, 46
Carlton House, 130
Caroline, Queen, 131
Carpenter, Charlotte, 66
Carr, John, 118, 125-126
Cavendish, William, Fifth Duke of Devonshire, 117-118, 126
Chamberlain, Neville, 55
Charles II, King, 23, 25
Chateau Impney (Droitwich), 63
Cheam, 182
Cheltenham, 34-39, 45-48, 54-55, 84-88, 116-117, 125, 155, 166-170, 178, 182
Cheltenham College, 47, 165-166, 167-168, 174
Cheltenham Ladies' College, 47, 53, 165, 169-170, 174
Cheltenham Literary Festival, 189
Cheltenham Races, 46
Chichester, 17
Children, 15, 97, 106
Cholera, 62
Christchurch Bay, 105
Christy Minstrels, 52
Church Stretton, 63-64, 114, 173, 181, 183
Cirencester (Glos), 156
City of London Collegiate School, 170
Clarke, Daniel, 176
Clarke, Paul, 177
Clerkenwell, 21
Clifton, 21, 31-32, 35, 84, 174
Clifton College, 174
Close, Rev. Francis, 45-48, 53-54, 165-166, 168-170
Cobbett, William, 154
Cole, Mary, 37
Collins, Tom, 101

Combe Down, 30, 80
Compressed Air Bath, 136, 138
Conference Centres, 183
Cork, 111
Cornwall, 79
Corpus Christi College, Oxford, 168
Cranston, James, 114
Craven Arms, 33
Cromer, 103, 112
Cromford (Derbys), 69
Cross Bath, 77
Currey, Henry, 118

Davies, Michael, 179
Davies, William, 88
Dawson, George, 51, 100-102
Deane, Edmund, 42
Dean Close Memorial School, 53, 171
Defoe, Daniel, 43, 109, 133
Derby Week, 26
Derrick, James, 79, 109
Deykes, John, 58-59
Dickens Charles, 138
Dobson, William, 47, 167
Douch, The, 60, 69, 135, 136
Dover Road, 112
Dragon School, Oxford, 172
Droitwich, 13, 17, 61-63, 98-100, 114, 117, 145, 174

East India Company, 151
Edward VII, King, 159-160
Electrotherapy, 60, 143
Elgar, Sir Edward, 181
Ellesmere College, Harrogate, 177
Epsom, 25-27, 74-75
Ergotherapy, 138, 143
Eton College, 90, 91
Evelyn, John, 21

Fairbourne Light Railway Co., 100
Faradisation, 143, 144

Fergusson, Dr J.N.F., 60
Farside, Robinson, 157-158
Fiennes, Celia, 20, 22, 72-74, 101, 146
Finishing Schools, 164
Flecker, James Elroy, 171
Flecker, Dr W.H., 170
Forbes, John, 116, 127
Ford, Rev. Edward, 171-172
Forth, William, 109
Fotheringham, Alexander, 155
Fox, Charles James, 153
Freeman, Alan, 123
French Revolution, 153

Galvanisation, 144
Gaming Act (1745), 79
Garrick, David, 23
Gay, John, 81
George III, King, 103, 105
George V, King, 110
Gilsand, 16, 66
Gloucester, 14
Goldsmith, Oliver, 31, 150
Greenaway, John, 120
Gulliver, Isaac, 106
Graffenburg, 135
Gully, Dr James Manby, 59-60, 134-136
Gwyn, Nell, 25

Hagley Hall (Worcs.), 81
Hammans, 111
Hanson, Charles, 172
Harcourt, Mary Countess of 59
Harlow Carr, 53
Harrogate, 11, 21, 22, 33, 34, 42-45, 50-56, 68, 74, 100-102, 104, 118-119, 133, 142, 159-160, 161, 176-177, 181, 182
Harrogate College, 177
Harrogate Hydropathic Company, 50
Hanover, 92, 93
Health Farms, 135

Health Foods, 135
Heliotherapy, 135
Henrietta Maria, Queen, 23, 149
Henry VIII, King, 18, 95
Holland, Henry, 130
Holt, 31, 173
Holywell (Flints.), 12, 18-19, 73
Hot Air Baths, 136
Hove, 128
Hughes, Neil, 136
Hughes, Thomas, 36
Hunter, William Bell, 97
Hyde Park Corner, 124
Hydropathy, 134-143

Infertility, 72, 149
Inhalatoria, 143
Ilkley, 145
Islington Spa, 21, 24

Johnson, Dr James, 58
Johnson, Dr Samuel, 23, 35, 109
Jones, Richard, 81

Kemp, Thomas Reade, 128
Kenilworth, 49
King, James, 36, 154
King James's Grammar School, Knaresborough, 176
Kings Bath, 77
Kingston on Thames, 182
Kingswood School, Bath, 175-176
Kilvert, Rev. Francis, 107
Knaresborough, 22, 34, 42, 74, 104, 175
Kursaal (Harrogate), 52, 55, 159, 160

Lamp Bath, 136
The Lancet, 140
Langland, William, 138
Lawn Tennis, 49
Lea and Perrins, 139
Lea Mills, 96

Leamington Spa, 35, 39-42, 48-
    50, 114, 117, 124
Lewes, 128
Link School, Malvern, 172
Lido, Droitwich, 63
Livingston, John, 26-27, 74-75
Llandrindod Wells, 32-33, 55
    65, 143, 161, 180-181, 183
Long Mynd, 64
Ludlow, 17, 64
Lunar Society, 88
Lutherell, Lady Anne, 107
Lygon, Frederick, 172
Lytton, Sir Edward Bulwer, 133

MacLeod, William, 134, 139
Madan, Dr Patrick, 24
Malvern, 50, 57-61, 68, 117, 136-
    139, 142, 171-173, 178,
    181, 182
Malvern College, 172-173, 174
Malvern Festival, 181
Malvern Seltzer Water, 139
Margate, 30, 103, 112, 152, 158
Margate Hoys, 112
Merino Suits, 97
Marshall, Captain, 117
Marshall, John, 137
Mason, William, 35, 85
Massage, 68, 111
Mathewes, Walter, 139
Matlock, 50, 69-70, 96-98, 117,
    137
Mayerne, Sir Theodore, 27
Melksham, 31-32, 115
Menuhin, Hepzibah, 181
Menuhin, Yehudi, 181
Merton College, Oxford, 57
Messel, Oliver, 122
Methodist Free Church, 70
Midland Railway Co., 69
Middle Temple, 76
Mildmay, Sir Henry, 92
Miller, William, 36
Mineral Water Hospital, Bath,
    84

Mohamed, Sake Deen, 110-111
Moreau, Simon, 36, 86-87
Mud Baths, 132
Mustard Baths, 97

Napoleon, 110
Napoleonic Wars, 110
Nash, John, 127-128, 130-131
Nash, Richard, 11, 29-31, 72,
    75-79, 82, 87, 91, 123, 146,
    148, 150-152
Nash, Dr Treadaway, 90, 129
Naturists, 135
Neckham, Alexander, 15
Negus, 158
Nesbitt, Edward, 158
Newark, 18
Noake, Rev. James, 176
North, Lord, 90

Old Smoaker, 107
Oliver, Dr William, 76
Otley (Yorks.), 96

Palladio, Andrea, 83
Palmer, John, 152-153
Papworth, John Buonarotti,
    116, 127
Pantiles, 24
Pate, Richard, 168
Pate's Grammar School, 48, 169
Paxton, Sir Joseph, 68
Phillips, Rev. Albert, 47, 187
Phillips, Dr Wilson, 58
Pepys, Samuel, 21, 26, 28
Pierrepoint, Henry, 92
Pitt, Joseph, 38-39, 117, 124, 128
Pitt, William, 81
Poole (Dorset), 106
Powick (Worcs.), 88
Pope, Alexander, 81
Preparatory Schools, 50-51, 166-
    167, 171-172, 173, 176,
    177-178, 182
Price, Simon, 137
Priestnitz, Vincenz, 59-60, 135

Prince of Wales, Frederick, 84
Prince Regent, George
     Augustus, 27, 40, 75, 93-
     95, 107, 124, 129, 131
Proctor, Anne, 170
Public Schools, 47, 54, 55, 65,
     90-91, 163-171, 172-173,
     174, 175-176, 178, 182
Pump Rooms, 44, 45, 49, 61, 66,
     67, 77, 113, 114-117, 118,
     119, 133

Radiation Treatment, 143
Rain Bath, 136
Ramsgate, 158
Redcar, 128
Reynolds, Sir Joshua, 25
Rheumatism, 35, 71, 133, 142
Ribber Castle, 97
Richardson's Charity School,
     177
Ripon, 115
Rotherham, 133
Royal Mail Coaches, 111
Royal School, Bath, 175
Royal Worcester Porcelain
     Company, 88
Rugby, 163
Rules of Conduct, 151-152, 157-
     158
Ruskin, John, 41
Russel, Richard, 106, 108

Sadler, Thomas, 21
Sadler's Wells, 21
Satchwell, Benjamin, 40
Saucimer, Sir Guy, 18
Salt Union, 99
Savery, G.M., 177
Scarborough, 34, 42, 103-105,
     157-158, 182
Scott, Gilbert, 178
Scott, Sir Walter, 66, 157
Scutt, Rev. Thomas, 128
Sham Castle, 81
Shanklin, 107

Shap Spa, 14
Shaw Bernard, 181
Shelsley Beauchamp, 114
Shergold, Samuel, 108
Shrewsbury, 64, 164
Skillicorne, Henry, 35, 43, 84, 86
Skillicorne, Rev. Richard, 86
Skillicorne, William, 35-36
Slingsby, William, 21
Smedley, Caroline, 97
Smedley, John, 69-70, 95-98,
     136-137, 157
Smollett, Tobias, 104
Southend on Sea, 112, 158
St Bride, 16
St Hugh's School, Woodhall
     Spa, 177
St Kenelm, 17
St Neot, 16
St Richard, 17
St Rumbold, 20
St Winifred, 18
Stanhope, Michael, 42
Steine, The, 106, 110
Stoke Prior, 98
Strahan, John, 20
Stratford-on-Avon, 49-50
Strutt, Isaac, 25, 118
Stray, The, 53
Sturmmes, Dr Leopold, 172
Stanhope, Lady Hester, 62
Sussex, University of, 178
Sykes, Christopher, 148
Sydenham, 21

Talyllyn Railway Co., 100
Taylor, Richard, 176
Tenbury Wells, 11, 61, 105, 173
Thackwray, Joseph, 44, 101
Temperance Societies, 156
Tippett, Sir Michael, 181
Towyn, 99-100
Tonbridge Wells, 20, 22-25, 29,
     56, 74, 114, 119, 124-125,
     129, 148-149, 178, 181, 182
Turner, David, 145

Turkish Baths, 111
Typhoid, 86

Vapour Baths, 68, 111, 136, 137
Vichy, 68

**Waguelin School of Russian
    Baller,** 178
Wall, Dr John, 57-58, 87-90
Wall, Martin, 58
Wakes Week, 159
Walsingham, 11, 18
Ward, Ned, 146-147
Warwick, 40, 49
Watkins, Nicholas, 139
Watt, James, 88
Webster, Captain, 29, 75-76
Welland Common, 59
Well Dressing, 12, 69, 70
Wellington, First Duke of, 38,
    41, 125, 131, 154
Well Walks, 43, 58, 74, 75, 140,
    149
Wesley, John, 175
Weymouth, 34, 103, 105-106

White, Thomas, 123
Wicker, Henry, 25
Wilds, Amon, 127-128
Wilds, Amon Henry, 125, 127-
    128, 129
Wilkes, John, 153
Wilkinson, John, 130
Willes, Rev. Edward, 41
William II, King, 15
William III, King, 24
William IV, King, 37, 95
Williams, John, 44
Williams, Stephen, 44
Wilson, Dr James, 59-60, 134-
    136
Wilson, James, 175
Wood, David, 129
Wood, John (The Elder), 30, 80,
    82-84
Wood, John (The Younger), 30,
    115, 119, 120-123
Woodhall Spa, 70-71, 177
Wookey Hole, 11
Worcester, 57-58, 88
Worcester Imfirmary, 58, 88, 89
Worthing, 105